Contents

PROLOGUE

"You were born in a hospital?' Hilde says as she lays down her black bread and cheese sandwich. She sits opposite me at my kitchen table.

Looking up from my salad, I nod. "Yes, I thought everyone by the 1940's was born in a hospital."

"Hell no," Hilde stares at me. "I was born at home on the couch delivered by a midwife."

Thus began the noontime discussions of an American housewife and a German cleaning lady about their contrasting lives during and after WWII.

My mother taught me that an important word in any language is while. While one thing is happening, so is another. "While I wash dishes, Peggy, you dry. While we are in nighttime, someone is in daylight. While one person dies, another is born."

With this word while we start this book. While a war was raging between the United States and Germany and World War II began, two little girls were growing up in opposing countries and living in its aftermath.

While Franklin Roosevelt was President of United States and Adolph Hitler, Chancellor of Germany, Germany declared war on America in late 1941.

In January 1941, Brunhilde Maria Maurer (Bruni) was born in Marktredwitz, Germany, the youngest child of three children who lived with her young mother and maternal grandmother while her father and grandfather fought in the war.

Four months earlier in September 1940, I Margaret Ruth Leis

(Peggy) was born in Aliquippa, Pennsylvania, in America, the only child of a music teacher and a banker serving the war on the home front.

While Bruni/Hilde and I discussed our growing up years, we agreed our vastly different experiences would make an interesting story. Years later, Bruni/Hilde handed me one hundred pages of handwritten notes about her life in Germany and America. I, Peggy, wrote about my life lived entirely in America from family notes and photos. Our voices as children of WWII appear in tandem sharing extreme contrasts and sometimes striking similarities.

Chapter One

1941-1945
Arzberg and Marktredwitz, Germany

While Britain and Allies bombed Germany to end Hitler's intent to control Europe and Britain, Brunhilde Maria Maurer was born and raised in southern Germany.

While sirens wailed.

Writhing on the dry ground, the screaming and crying boy glowed. Allied planes had passed over our neighborhood and dropped phosphorus bombs. An exploded bomb sprayed the boy who dropped to the ground in pain. He crawled inside the root cellar, *Luftbunker,* our air raid shelter. Sirens stopped. Neighbors ran passing him on their way to safety. No one dared touch the boy, not even his wailing mother who was held from him by old women. "*Nicht anfassen!* Don't touch", they said. Touching the silver substance could be fatal. The mother stood staring at him, torn between loving and living. Terrified, her son reached out to her. She shook her head and screamed, "*Mein sohn!* My son!" Phosphorus, the burning agent, spread along his body and scorched his clothes. He rolled in the dirt to smother it. "*Mutti, Mutti,* Mommy, Mommy", he called as his blackened flesh began to curl.

My mother dragged me passed the boy. Scared, I stumbled after her my small hand held tightly in hers. Mothers carrying small children shielded little faces from the hideous sight. *Omas*, grandmothers, prayed, "*Mein Got in Himmel*". We huddled in the back of the root

1

cellar, away from him. In the dark we noticed a small splash of glowing phosphorus on my mother's clothes. It burned a hole in her jacket, but did not reach her skin. Women ripped off her jacket and buried it in the corner of the cellar.

That night the boy died alone. I recognized him from the neighborhood and felt sorry for him. He was nine-years-old, an only child whose father was in the *Armee*. Although I was only three, forever, I will see his glowing death.

Earlier that sunny afternoon, Mom and I were lying on top of a wooden shed enjoying the warmth and peacefulness surrounding us. We were staying with my *Oma* in Arzberg. Suddenly a loud roaring came from the sky. "Come quickly," Mom said as she jumped down, grabbed my hand and dragged me across the courtyard into the underground root cellar. "I don't want to go, again" I yelled, but Mom could see the rising smoke from the firestorm beyond where Allied planes had dropped bombs. "We must" she said. "Planes are coming here this time." We had daily air raids and nighttime black-outs, windows covered with blankets and house police patrolling for darkness. "How long will we hide?" I asked trying to keep up with her.

"This is not a drill," she yelled over the screams of the neighbors who came running from their homes carrying and pulling crying children. Old men hobbled behind us shouting "Hurry! Don't crowd." Women appeared wearing *Kopftücher*, head scarves, and full aprons, pockets bulging with candle stubs. Scrambling down into the dark damp cellar, Mom and I found a place to sit among piles of rotting cabbages and potatoes. "It smells bad," I said. "I want out of here."

The door to the cellar was shut. Black dust settled on us. We were hiding again.

All night, we stayed under the eerie silence from outside, waiting for the repeating rumblings from the plane's bombs. Old women gossiped, "Did you hear about..." Young mothers nursed infants "Don't be afraid, my child." Children sat in laps of strangers. Lighted candle stubs became our only light. We drank water stored in jugs filled after the last raid. Upturned empty crates became our seats. An old man brought an accordion and softly played "Liechtensteiner Polka", waltzes and familiar folk songs.

Covered with musty blankets stored in the cellar, we slept on top of the hard potatoes and curled up among the cabbages. No other place was usable. "I want my bed," I moaned. Mothers crooned lullabies. Children sobbed. Old women told stories of better days. My mother stood up and walked in a circle. "I need to stretch my legs to keep from cramping," she said. Older children begged "Please can we go out now?" Staying in such cramped quarters was boring and scary. But seeing the boy's death reminded us of the dangers above.

Hearing the sirens wail all-clear, slowly we filed out of the cellar skirting the blackened body at the door. "Who does these bad things to us?" I asked as we headed for the wooden door. Opened, bright sunlight blinded us after the darkness of our hiding place. Blinking, we staggered back to our homes. "Still standing," everyone whispered in thanksgiving as they approached their homes. Dark smoke in the sky behind told us that the city of Arzberg was burning. China factories where townspeople worked had been bombed and, perhaps, destroyed. "Why, do the bombs come, *Mutti*?" I asked.

A newcomer to the village reported that in cities every evening at six, families gathered blankets, flashlights and water to descend into public concrete bunkers. Children following their parents would ask, "Why do we do this every night?" Nighttime bombings in cities such as Berlin were constant. Whistling in the air indicated incoming bombs, then silence, followed by violent explosions. "Did they hit our house?" children asked. "When will they stop?" was everyone's unanswered question. After the all-clear sirens, people re-emerged into a city not knowing what destruction awaited. They had folded their blankets on cots or murmured thanks to the stranger seated next to them on the wooden benches. Ascending the steps, they entered a world where bricks blown from a nearby building lay at odd angles across a sidewalk, crushed glass glistened in piles of leaves under an empty window frame, a red wagon balanced high in the "v" of tree branches. Every return to the neighborhoods brought new scenes of destruction.

Out in our open areas, Allied planes dropped tin foil strips which drifted down to interfere with German radar. Floating strips made weird clattering sounds and filled the sky with metal. Mornings after a night raid, neighborhood children and I would run among them. "Catch on as many shiny strips as you can." We would run with our hands in the air. "Bang them into each other." Kicking the strips on the ground, we'd call, "Stomp on them."

***

My *Vater* Ludwig and my grandfather Simon served in the German Army during the war. My *Oma,* grandmother, Maria and my mother Elise, took care of me, my sister Anneliese, nine years older and my brother Helmut, three years older. My brother and I were born at home in Marktredwitz delivered by a midwife. My sister was born in Arzberg and lived there with *Oma.* We were named from a list of acceptable names posted by Hitler. He wanted sophisticated names for the German people.

Mother, Helmut and I lived on the second floor of a two story apartment house in Marktredwitz where my parents lived when my father went off to war. We lived in two bedrooms and a kitchen above a fruit and vegetable store on the main street of the town, a pedestrian plaza.

When I was a baby, I had no toys. My mother put me on the floor in front of a full-length mirror. I watched myself in the mirror, entertaining myself for hours. Our apartment had beautiful hardwood floors. Mom would wash and wax them weekly. "Now you can polish the floors," she would say to Helmut and me when I was older. She put socks and towels on our feet and told us to glide back and forth until the floor was shiny. It felt like gliding on ice.

I had a lonely childhood. When I did play with my brother, I always got in trouble. One time we were tossing a potato. Helmut stood in front of a window. "Catch," I called and threw the potato to him. He ducked. The potato went through the glass. "You moved!" I yelled, but I was blamed for the broken window. "We have no money to replace it," my mother cried. She spanked me, not my brother.

***

Food was limited during the war. In my growing up years, we starved for months and ate only *Schwarzbrot*, black bread. Some bread was made from ground tree bark and flour. With no margarine or butter, we ate bread with sugar on top sprinkled with water to keep the

4

sugar from falling off. Everyone lived on rations, but Mom would think of things to cook, sometimes we had potatoes only. She would slice them and bake them, or she would mix flour and milk and eggs together and bake pancakes in a pan. When she had milk, she would heat it and put pieces of *schwarzbrot* into the milk. That was our supper or breakfast.

We stayed often with my *Oma*, in Arzberg. She held our family together. Some days, she would take a bag and metal pitcher and leave. "Where are you going? Can I go, too?" I'd ask hoping this day she'd take me. She would shake her head "Be a good girl and wait for me." She'd walk two kilometers, about one and a quarter miles, one way to a farm to barter her beautiful paintings and china, silverware and hand-made embroidered linens for milk, eggs and bread. We drank water and coffee. Coffee was made with roasted barley seeds, grains or acorns. (1)

With rationing, every day *Oma* would go into town. "Why do you take a brown card?" I asked *Oma*. "It lets me get food," she said. "I must stand in line for a long time." Many days she came home without food. "They were all sold out by my turn."(2)

Cards were used with *Marken*, stamps with printed values. Appropriate *Marken* were needed for bread, cheese, fats, eggs, jams and sugar when available. Vegetables and fruits were not rationed. Men working in heavy industry received heavy rations. POWs were brought to Germany to work in the armament industry and agriculture. (3)

Farmers let us come into the fields, miles from *Oma's* apartment, to glean the last of the potatoes and beets. Women gathered potatoes in their aprons, the same people who hid from air raids with us scurried about the dry fields. Bonfires were built. "Throw the potatoes in," the adults would shout. "Let them cook, then dig them out with sticks." Children would chase each other around the fires while the potatoes baked. "They're ready." Someone would yell. "Be careful. They are very hot."

Potatoes, cabbages, rutabagas, beets and any other vegetables we found and boiled were sometimes the day's only meal. Some women saved and bundled vegetable peelings to trade with farmers for rabbit meat and pork. Peelings were used for animal food. Fat from bones was made into soaps, so we could wash ourselves and our clothes.

Oma lived in an apartment complex shaped like a "U" enclosing a courtyard on three sides and opening to the woods on the fourth. The landlord lived in an apartment over the entrance across the front. Two massive wooden doors at street level opened for cars and people to enter. Two floors of apartments formed the side buildings. *Oma's* apartment was in the back of the east side on the first floor. The shed my mother and I were sunbathing on was in back of her building and the root cellar under the west building. A doctor lived in the complex. He had a car, an Opel, and would drive in through the doors. "Give us a ride," we children would shout. He would stop and give us a ride into the garage under his apartment.

We liked to stay at *Oma's*. The landlord was good to the renters. At Easter, he and his daughters would hide eggs in the woods beyond for the children to find. In the fall he would hold a *Schlachtfest,* a pig roast for all. At Christmas time he raised a huge decorated outdoor pine tree. There was a restaurant to the left of the wooden entry doors.(4)

***

"Der Führer kommt! The *Führer* is coming!" One day during the war, the news spread through Arzberg. Hitler, the father of our country, was coming to see his people. We could go to the center of town and greet him. The leader of Germany and his entourage would be passing through. To see *Den Führer* was exciting. More people than I ever saw lined the street. Holding red flags with a black *Swastika* centered in a white circle, we waited and waited.

Suddenly the roar of motorcars filled the air. Shouts of *"Heil Hitler!"* came from our left. As a small child, I was pushed to the front of the crowd. My mother said it was important to see this man, so I stood with other children and waved my little flag. Many big black cars roared by with Nazi flags on front. "Here he comes!" people around me yelled. With one arm outstretched, they saluted proudly calling *"Sieg Heil"* And there he was! In an open car, a man in a black uniform stood at attention and returned their salute. He had a small black mustache and looked so strong. Sunshine gleamed off the gold buttons of his uniform as he stood looking straight ahead. As part of the crowd lining the street, I jumped up and down, screamed and yelled with them. I had seen *Den Führer!*

***

One morning in Arzberg, around ten o'clock, my mother, brother and I took a walk. There was a man with my mother. "Who is this man?" Helmut and I asked each other. "His name is Robert," my mother answered. He was my mother's lover.

Robert pushed a bicycle. I sat on the handlebar. Helmut sat on the rack on the back of the bike over the rear wheel. My mother and Robert were talking and giggling. It was peaceful all around us with the warm morning sun shining and birds singing. Surrounded by trees, we strolled on a small path wide enough for two or three people. On the left, flowed a river. High up on its bank ran the railroad. Helmut called, "Bruni" over the valley and I heard my name echo. The trail lined with hazelnut trees and wildflowers went on and on with bends at the right side. We came to a long building surrounded by a fence and a main gate. Walking through that valley many times later as a teenager the memories of that day came back to me as if it happened yesterday.

POP, POP, POP.

My mother screamed, "What's happening?" Robert stopped and tried to hold the bicycle upright. With the wobbling bike and children sitting on it, he didn't know what to do. He dropped the bike. "Help!" My brother yelled as he landed about ten feet down the hill near the river. I fell on the walk, "*Mutti*", I cried.

As suddenly as the popping sounds rang out, they stopped. All of us were screaming. "Bruni," my mother called. "Are you all right?" she asked as she reached for me, her hands shaking. Robert climbed down the hill to pick up my bleeding brother. "I'm hurt. I'm hurt," he screamed.

My mother and Robert knelt beside us saying, "It's all right. *Mutti's* here." With shock and horror, my mother realized that the popping had come from a gun, a rifle or a pistol. She recognized the shooter. "Ludwig, it is you!" she screamed. Her husband, my *Vater*, was shooting at us! When he did not succeed in hitting us, he took off running. I never saw him. He was not charged with any crime. My mother did not know that my *Vater* had come home from the war on furlough and waited for us behind the nail factory. He meant to kill us or scare my mother and Robert.

That incident changed my mother's life.

My *Vater* had found out about my mother and Robert, came home and followed us. He turned my mother in to the SS *Schutzwaffe*, German for Protective Squadron. The SS arrested my mother and sent her to a concentration camp. Robert was a Ukraine prisoner of war sent to work in the fields. "Ours was called False Love," my mother said later. Consorting with a prisoner of war was *verboten*, by Hitler. Germans were not permitted to date or associate with prisoners. Hitler gave orders to hang Robert.

So my mother vanished for a long time. Helmut and I were sent to live with *Oma* and Anneliese in Arzberg. "Where did she go?" I kept asking *Oma*. "When is she coming back?" Waiting seemed like a lifetime to me. Nighttimes, I'd cry, "I want *Mutti*." I was too young to understand why she left me.

While Mother was in Ravensbrück, the concentration camp, she met other German women from our town who had also become involved with prisoners of war. My mother and four other women decided to escape the horrible treatment and the terrible things they witnessed. "In the dark of night, we tied sheets and blankets together, dropped them outside a window and let them fall to the ground," she said. "We slid down the rope. When it was my turn, the sheets opened and I lost my grip and fell to the ground." With painful bruises on her body, Mother escaped to a church and stayed overnight. Somehow she came home by train and arrived the next night. My grandmother let my mother into the house and hid her behind an armoire in the bedroom.

It did not take very long for the German *Gestapo* to arrive and pull my mother out of her hiding place. "A neighbor had seen me come home and vanish into the house." Mother said. "She reported me." In the war there were some German people who would report anyone to receive a bowl of soup. Afraid of severe punishment from the Nazis, anyone would turn people in to save their own skin or protect their families.

The SS returned my mother back into Ravensbrück. "She came and left again. Why?" I would ask *Oma,* but she never explained.

***

One night when I was about four years old, I walked to the train station with my grandmother, my brother and sister. My Aunt Emile, Uncle Paul and their two children were arriving. I had never met my mother's sister's family. "Tell me who they are again." *Oma* explained that they were living on a farm in eastern Germany. The Russians were taking over that part of Germany, seizing all the people's farms.

Fleeing the Russians, Aunt Emile, Uncle Paul with my cousin Ingrid and Baby Hannelore were coming to live with us. "You're safe now," *Oma* cried as she hugged each one of them. I stood alone and watched my grandmother welcome strangers. "There is no housing available. They will live with us in our apartment," *Oma* said. Eight of us lived in the apartment. With not enough beds, some slept on burlap stuffed with straw. Everyone caught head lice.

When my mother returned from Ravensbrück, she wore a shiny green skirt and jacket. She knelt before me and put her arms around me and asked, "Do you know who I am?" I looked at her and said, "No." Mom started crying. Tears ran down her cheeks behind her glasses. After she rested for a few weeks, we went back to our apartment in Marktredwitz.

Vater, home from the war, didn't live with us. He lived in town with his mother and brother. I met my father's mother, my Grandmother Therese, then. A small, spry woman she lived with Uncle Andreas on the third floor of an old house. Short and chubby with a lovely round face and lively eyes, she always embraced me when I came to visit her. Mom told me to ask her to ask my *Vater* for some money. In the back of my mind, I knew I should be seeing my grandfather, Thomas, too, but it dawned on me that maybe he was dead.

One day I asked my grandmother about him. She explained that she and Thomas were born in Austria. He served under the Emperor Franz Joseph in WWI. After the war the family fled to Germany. Grandfather Thomas was a glassblower. He died before I was born. Three of my father's brothers died in the War. Four sons survived and lived to an old age. Grandmother Therese was nice, not at all like my *Vater.*

Our apartment was in the back of a building with a balcony overlooking the backyard surrounded by a stone wall. We entered the building from a side alley which continued onto the school and church beyond. Many times I would go across the street to the huge Catholic Church and sit inside because it was so beautiful and peaceful. On Saturdays, from my side of the street, I would watch the happy brides and grooms come out. "Why don't we go to this church?" I would ask.

Mother explained that we were Lutherans. Our family didn't go to church, but we observed Christmas. With no money for presents, we celebrated with *Stollen*, Christmas bread, cookies and a live tree decorated with lighted candles.

White trimmed windows, a red roof and red cornerstones outlined our white stone apartment building which sat on the plaza sandwiched between the police station and city hall. Benches in front of the building faced the center of town. Small dormers peeked out from the roof and cupola with windows and a pointed red roof sat atop the building. We could always hear, "*Guten Morgan,*Good Morning, *Guten Nachmittag,* Good Afternoon, *or Guten Abend"* Good Evening, everyday from the townspeople seated on benches in front of our building.

A large fountain rose from the middle of the town square. One day I tied a little wooden wagon to my dog, Teddy's tail. Wild with fear and barking loudly, he ran into the town square, running around and around and barking loudly, dragging and bumping the wagon over the cobblestones. "Look at that dog!" Everyone stopped to watch and laughed at him running in circles around the fountain. "Teddy, come," I'd call. Finally, he came back to me.

I saw my mother coming towards me saying, "What's going on out here?" I thought my mother would spank me, but she laughed too.

One day after the war, Mom told Helmut and me that we could go to a flea market on the main street. In those days it was safe for children to roam all over town without an adult. "Hold my hand," Helmut said as we walked around the flea market looking at things. "Can we buy some candy or ice cream?" I'd say. "Quiet," he'd say. "You know we have no money." While we were watching people, suddenly my brother said "Don't let go of my hand!" He was talking to a man I did not know. Helmut was about nine and I was about six. He knew the man was Ludwig, our *Vater.* The man approached me holding a cane. *Vater* placed his fingers in the corners of his mouth and pull his lips apart to make a horrible face. Distorted, it frightened us. "Helmut, make him stop," I screamed. My brother backed away, gripping my hand. *Vater* followed us. A short man, he bent right into our faces. Helmut jerked my arm, started running and shouting "Get away from us!" I stumbled after him screaming. "Who is that mean man?"

When we arrived home, Helmut blurted "*Mutter, Mutter, Vater* was at the flea market and he made horrible faces at us. I ran home with Bruni as fast as I could. *Vater* really scared us."

That was the first time I saw my *Vater*. He had never come to see us, never sent us gifts or money. One time my mother came home very upset. "Your *Vater* raised his cane to strike me in public," she said. "When I ran, he threw the cane at me." My *Vater* hated her for what she had done to him when she had an affair with Robert. Although my *Vater* had extramarital affairs also and received love letters from other women, he could not understand or tolerate his wife betraying him while he was at war.

When my *Vater* was told to pay child support, he quit his full time job. He only worked part time and told the court he could not afford to pay child support. My mother finally gave up fighting for that money and divorced him. She had to go on welfare and received very little money.

My mother brought another man home. Mother took him in as a boarder and he slept on a sofa in the kitchen. Again, my brother and I wondered aloud, "Who is this man?" Wadek Wadislow Kubarski could speak very little German. Polish and displaced or kidnapped by the Nazis, he was sent to Germany. He became Mother's lover and continued to live with us.

"Why is he nice to you and not us?" Helmut and I asked. Mother just smiled. Wadek automatically assumed the role of *Vater*. "He's not our father!" we'd say. Mother smiled again. She let him beat us, not so much me, but he had it in for my brother. My mother had been lenient with my brother. "I will make a man," Wadek said in broken German.

We were starving. One night Wadek and his Polish friends stole a cow, killed it in the woods, cut it into pieces, and brought it home. Mom cut smaller pieces and cooked it. Mother gave portions to our neighbors to keep them from reporting Wadek. The hallway of our second floor was lined with the families' huge armoires. The German police came the next day looking for the meat. They never found it. Neighbors had hidden the meat in their armoires and ate well for a long time.

Another night Wadek went with friends to steal apples. They returned with baskets full of beautiful green apples. Another day they returned with tires. They were cut up and used to burn in the stove. We had no wood or coal. The entire neighborhood stunk of burning rubber. That must have tipped off the German police.

While Germany and its families were recovering from the war, it was time for me to start school. I had no idea what was to come.

Chapter Two

1940-1945
Aliquippa, Pennsylvania, America

While war raged in Europe, Pearl Harbor was bombed and the United States entered war, Peggy was born and raised in the States.

While sirens wailed.

I sat cross-legged sandwiched between the white Kelvinator refrigerator with its hat box motor and the doorway to the cellar, my back against the wall under the family's jackets on coat hooks, dressing and undressing my wooden doll. "You know, Suzi Q, we have to stay here," I said putting on her shoes and socks." Until we hear the sirens stop and start again. We're safe here in our corner," I said hugging my companion. "We aren't afraid, are we?"

Across the dimly lit room, Mother and her mother, Grandma Craig, sat at the kitchen table, the window above covered with a dark blanket. Seated at one side of the table, Mother looked up from playing Solitaire saying, "We won't be here much longer. It will soon be bedtime." Grandma opposite her, stroking her tiny Chihuahua Skippy on her lap, sang "On a hill faraway stood an old rugged cross" from one of her beloved hymns. We were in a black-out in the midst of an air raid drill.

My dad patrolled the neighborhood as an air raid warden. Over the age limit to serve as a soldier on the battle front, he proudly served his country on the home front.(5)

13

Dad wore a white helmet. "Can I try it on?" I would ask. It wobbled on my small head. Daytimes I strutted around the house shining a flashlight on windows, "You need to cover your window," I would say to my pretend neighbor. Dad's flashlight lit his way up and down the dark street until the all-clear siren sounded. Windows of lighted rooms were to be covered in homes along our street, street lights were out, no lights were to be seen. I wasn't afraid during a drill. I was at home with my mother and my father was protecting us.

Air raid drills were held frequently in my hometown. "Why here?" I asked not sensing any danger. My dad explained, "Although we live inland near Pittsburgh, we could be a target for the enemy. The steel mills in Aliquippa produce steel for the war."

But the war was far away. I felt safe.

My parents, grandparents, aunts and uncles and their families told me many stories of living with civilian effects of WWII. Food and supplies were limited in wartime by the government Office of Price Administration and Civilian Supply. Rationing was imposed. "We signed up at local schools for stamp books filled with twenty-eight color coded postage size coupons." Warnings on stamp books read: NEVER BUY RATIONED GOODS WITHOUT RATION STAMPS. NEVER PAY MORE THAN THE LEGAL PRICE. (6)

The first nonfood item rationed was rubber. With no rubber for new tires, most people used public transportation, walked or rode bikes. Trains were reserved for troop transport. No new cars were made. My parents drove a grey 1940 Plymouth for many years. To me, it looked like "a hump back whale". The car had a letter B sticker on the lower right side of the passenger side front window. This indicated the gallon allowances of gas depending on owner's occupation. Mother drove Dad to the bank one day a week, so she could have the car. "Our day for shopping," she'd say putting me as a child into the car. "Sit still, and watch out the window." I'd sit beside her in a child's canvas car seat hung over the front seat.

My cousins told me foil from gum wrappers, candy bars and cigarette packages were saved and turned in to be melted down for the wartime effort. People spent white pennies made of zinc coated steel because copper and nickel were needed for the wartime effort. Empty toothpaste tubes were exchanged for new ones. My Aunt Alice made delicious eggless cakes and a friend made moist cakes from tomato soup. Meatless Mondays and Heatless Tuesdays were instituted to conserve meat and energy.

Mother said that with rations, it was difficult to cook three different meals daily. "It was hard to make these meals appetizing," she told me. She cooked meat and potatoes for my working father and growing me, a soft diet for aging Grandma Craig and a bland/ulcer diet for herself, a nervous person who had ulcers and migraine headaches.

Grandma and Granddad Leis lived in town and grew a "Victory Garden" in their backyard. Labor and transportation shortages made it hard to harvest and move fruits and vegetables to market. My granddad bought seeds at the local hardware store. Gardens were planted in backyards, empty lots, ball fields and city rooftops. Granddad Leis grew onions, radishes, lettuce, beans and tomatoes in his backyard. "Onion sets must be in by St. Patrick's Day," was his motto. Strings wound around stakes outlined the rows. Empty seed packs perched on the sticks named the row of vegetables. Every Sunday when we visited, I would see the plants growing into different shapes.

Grandma would call "Who wants to help me with the beans?" She and I would sit on the back porch steps, Grandma in her full apron with a bowl of beans in her lap, me on the step below. We would "snap" fresh green beans. The "one, two, three" rhythm of snapping off each end, then snapping the bean in half stays with me.

Housewives were encouraged to can vegetables to save commercial canned goods for the troops. "Don't touch the hot jars," Mother said wearing a huge apron covering her clothes and big pot holders on her hands. "The jars have been sterilized." Mason jars, Ball rubber rings and heavy glass lids with wire locks sat on a towel drying. The kitchen grew extremely hot from the end of summer heat, sterilized jars, and cooked vegetables packed in jars.

"Stay out of my way!' Mother would say as she carried jars from the sink to the stove and back again. I would scamper back to my seat on the steps and watch, fascinated by the process. A huge blue and white speckled enameled canning pot with its wire basket inside sat on the stove holding the sealed and packed Mason jars in a hot water bath. After all were removed and cooled, they were stored in a pantry at the bottom of the cellar steps, the shelves then filled with Mother's canned tomatoes, carrots, beans, jams and jellies.

Mother made jams and jellies from the nearby blackberry bushes. She bought other fruits and vegetables from "truck farmers" who brought their produce to town, stopped on each street, and sold produce from the back of their trucks. In our kitchen, cheesecloth bags hung over the counters. Tied with string and hung from knobs of the cupboards over the counter, each bag sagged and strained the cooked berries into bowls. After sugar was added, the jam or jelly was poured into small jars and sealed with paraffin wax. A metal two piece lid screwed on top. My dad always teased her asking "What ARE you doing? This kitchen looks like a barn with rows of full cow udders."

Goods and services were delivered. The dry cleaner picked up and delivered my dad's suits and left a bill at the end of the month. Bakery trucks delivered bread to our door. Milkmen left glass bottles of milk on doorsteps or in metal boxes. Our milkman Joe, our neighbor, replaced empty bottles Mother left out the night before. Mother might leave a note "Need cream today" and he would add a small bottle to the order on the side steps.

The side steps into our house formed a "danger zone". Three outside steps led to a cement stoop, with a roof, outlined by white lattice sides covered with ivy. All led to the side door. We entered the house onto a landing, immediately taking three more steps up into the kitchen or sixteen steps to the right down to the cellar. In good weather Dad sat on the steps drinking his morning coffee. He'd bring in the glass bottles of milk and return to the sunshine with his coffee cup. "Be careful," one of many warnings called out to anyone entering or leaving by the side door. "Watch your step."

When a child I had a recurring dream of falling down the sixteen steps from that landing. In the dream, I have lost my footing, and balancing on the top step, lose my grip on the door knob and fall backwards. No one hears my cries of "Help!" Arms flailing, I tumble into the abyss until I'd force myself awake.

Our house was a three bedroom white frame "two story" on Polk Street, the fourth level of Sheffield Terrace. Married two years, my parents bought the newly built house in 1937. Mother, thirty-five, had been teaching music in public schools for twelve years. Dad, thirty-three, had been in banking for eight years. "My goal is to have the house furnished before we start a family," my mother stated. She accomplished her goal. I was born three years later into a fully furnished household.

A porch ran the full length of the front of the house, shaded in summer by green and white striped awnings. My bedroom and my parent's bedroom windows overlooked the porch roof. In my teen years when Mother and I had an argument about my messy room, she'd threaten, "I'll take the door off, so God and everybody can see your mess." Angry, I'd counter, "Then I'll climb out the window and tell everybody that you took the door off!"

Downstairs, the living room spread across the front of the house. Sitting in the middle of the front wall, the door flanked by two windows opened onto the porch. The doorbell made a terrible BUZZ that always scared me. Sometimes Mother saw a door-to-door salesman come onto our porch, pass the window and approach the door. "Come stand by me behind this wall so he can't see us", she'd say. "Pretend we're not home. I don't want to buy what he's selling."

Jackson, Van Buren, Tyler, Polk, Fillmore, Pierce, Buchanan… I could name some of the presidents from the street names on Sheffield Terrace. (I never knew why some were omitted.) The Terrace sat away from the main part of town. Most families with men working in the mill lived closer to the mill. Houses on The Terrace were built on streets lining the hillside divided by Grand Avenue and Division Street.

As a child of the war, my life was touched by rationing, air raid drills and two soldiers.

A large photo of my Aunt Rene's fiancé, Mel, serving in the army, sat on her dresser at my grandparent's. He was in a United States Army uniform leaning toward the camera with a patch on his sleeve of a big red one. "Why that number?" I asked.

My Aunt Rene proudly said, "He served with the First Division under General Patton in Africa". When he came home, he and my dad's sister were married. I was five-years-old and a flower girl in their wedding, feeling very grown-up wearing my first long dress.

I saw our next door neighbor's son when he came home from the United States Air Force on furlough. I would ask his mother "Why do you cry when you see him?" She'd shake her head and say, "You'll know someday." Photos show Russ in uniform squatting with three-year-old me and his black cocker spaniel, Lady.

***

When Mother and I went to the movies, we watched black and white ten minute Pathos or Movietone newsreels of WWII before the feature film, of soldiers on D Day and The Battle of the Bulge. The newsreels always started with a rooster crowing. I would always ask, "What does a rooster have to do with the war?"

"Lassie" called by a boy's voice started popular films of a boy and his collie. My mother had to take me out of my seat and into the lobby when Lassie and Timmy were in danger. "They're going to get hurt," I'd sob out loud. "Lassie will be OK, Peggy," she'd say kneeling in front of me. "This is a movie. Lassie always gets home. Let's go back in and watch."

Evenings, my parents and relatives sat around the Philco radio console listening to battle reports. "This is Edward R. Morrow reporting from London." My dad read the daily newspapers with front page maps and followed battle locations from lines and arrows on printed maps.

I grew up celebrating birthdays with parties. Mother saved eggs for birthday cakes during the war. Photos of my third birthday party show eight girls standing in front of our house. Each holds a glass Coke bottle filled with sand and dressed beautifully as a doll, door stops my mother had made for favors. For my fifth birthday party, many children sit at a long picnic table in our garage as my mother's friends served us. Everyone is wearing a party hat and eating a cupcake.

My best friend, Carolee, a year younger, and her family lived to the east side of our house. We could call each other across the driveway from our open bedroom windows on the second floors. "Carolee, are you there?" I would call. Or I'd hear, "Peggy, where are you?" We played together almost daily. Movies show the two of us hanging doll clothes on low clothes lines, eating peanut butter and jelly sandwiches outdoors at a small picnic table and cooling off from hot summer suns splashing in tin washtubs with other neighborhood kids. In photos, Carolee and I posed each winter sitting on sleds, bundled in matching coats and leggings, in spring, sporting light coats and straw Easter hats, and summers wearing one piece bathing suits and in fall, buttoned-up in sweaters and colorful head scarves.

The kitchen windows of our two houses faced each other. Our mothers gave an "OK" sign to each other at the end of the day when Carolee and I were finally bedded down for the night. Summer nighttimes, we could hear Pittsburgh Pirates baseball games and updates of the war coming from the radio in Rittelman's kitchen and see her mother, Betty, ironing clothes in nighttime coolness. Mother's radio played classical music all day. She ironed mornings, seated on a high stepstool at an ironing board in her bedroom. "Why do you sit?" I'd ask oblivious to her back problems.

In our kitchen, the refrigerator sat beside my play space and the door down to the outside. On the adjoining wall, in the stove Mother created a "warming oven". When Dad would be late coming home from the bank because "money didn't balance", traffic was bad or he had a meeting, she'd put a plate of food in the storage drawer for pots and pans. We ate breakfasts and lunches at a small steel topped table extended out from a kitchen window. Evening meals were always eaten in the dining room.

***

Some summer weekends, Mother and Dad and I would drive an hour and a half to my Uncle John's farm. My mother's brother and his wife Aunt Alfretta had a small farm up the hill from their main house in northwestern Pennsylvania. The farmhouse bedroom where I slept was heated from the register in the kitchen ceiling. Serving double duty, it sent up heat and voices from the kitchen below. I loved falling asleep to the rising voices and waking to the smell of coffee and cinnamon rolls.

A long, hilly road ran from the main road to the house and barn. Clouds of dust arising from it announced "Someone's coming!" My cousins, Patty, Paul and I and rode on a tractor driven by Uncle John's daughters, Florence and Helen Louise. "Put us on Nellie," we'd say and ride the old white nag around the farm. There, we spent days in a different world.

Evenings in the main house, Uncle John's deep booming voice filled the house when he sang "Nearer My God to Thee" and other Protestant hymns while he played an old pump organ. "Keep pumping," he'd say to Patty and Paul and me. We sat on the floor pumping the pedals to keep the organ playing. Around the corner, a deer head was mounted on the wall at the foot of the stairs. Its huge rack of antlers and big eyes seemed all-knowing and scared me. I would scurry up and down the steps not looking at the head. In later years, Florence and Helen Louise traveled the world. Evenings at Uncle John's main house, we "traveled" from their slides and narrations.

***

Back home, Carolee and I were inseparable.

"Let's play barbershop," we said one day when were about four and five-years-old. We went into the garage and shut the door. I had the scissors "How short do you want it cut?" Carolee shrugged her shoulders. I began cutting and cut off all her red corkscrew curls. I can still see our mothers facing each other afterwards. Her mother stood on the steps in our house, feet apart, hands on her hips. Carolee stood in front of her with clumps of red standing up in a bad crew cut. "See what your daughter did!" her mother wailed.

I stood behind my mother. "Peggy how could you?" my mother screamed. Both women cried. Carolee and I couldn't understand their tears.

"We were just playing," we said. We were both punished. Anywhere we went together after that incident, I was introduced as "The girl who cut Carolee's hair". It was embarrassing. To make matters worse, Carolee's hair never grew in curly.

The two of us were known as the best dressed little ladies in the neighborhood. It was not unusual to see us wearing our mother's clothes clunking down the street in their high heels, wearing huge hats and carrying big purses. We knocked on neighbors' doors on our side of the street. "Hello," we'd say. "Can you tell who we are?" We weren't allowed to cross the street, so we always knocked on the same doors.

A vacant lot sat between our house and Paines, the neighbors to the west. My parents and the Paines bought the land and shared cutting the grass. We had neighborhood and church picnics in the open lot. Mother would cook corn on the cob in washtubs in our cellar and pass them out on trays through the cellar window. The rest of the meal was pot luck for whoever attended. One picnic honored a missionary who had just returned from a foreign land. We'd gather around him after the meal and he'd say, "Do you know that children in ...?" I was fascinated with his stories of how children lived somewhere else.

One day Carolee and I, tired of dressing up, decided to play Leap Frog. Standing in the middle of the vacant yard, a large wooden frame held a tightly stretched wet lace curtain. Our continuous leaps over each other's backs sent us through the neighbor's white lace. "Look what you did," she yelled. Panicked, we looked back at the ragged hole we'd made. "We'll pay for it," we said running home. Carolee and I emptied our piggy banks. Forty-nine pennies didn't help pay for antique lace!

As Polk Street children, we knew to play quietly during the days as most men on our street worked different shifts at the steel mill. We didn't know whose father might be sleeping daytimes and working third shift at night. "Look at the window," was our motto. Usually a drawn bedroom window blind was our signal to play away from that house.

During the war, town's men stayed on the home front working in the mill producing rolled steel to build ship hulls, tank armor and other weapons. The Aliquippa plant of J&L Steel proudly displayed a Navy award for production during the war.

Holiday dinners at Grandma and Granddad Leis' were always scheduled around my aunt and uncles' mill schedules. Sometimes we had two main meals. My cousins and I didn't mind, but it meant a lot of work for my grandma and aunts.

"Who gets to sit at the adult table?" My cousins and I would count the number of adults. Our advancement to the adult table happened if someone moved away, went to college or became an adult. Most of the Leis relatives, Aunt Alice who lived with Grandma and Granddad, Aunt Leola (Ola) and her two boys, Aunt Clara and Uncle Joe and their four children, Aunt Rene and Uncle Mel and their two children stayed in the area, so cousins continued to sit at the children's table. My cousin Ed made it to the adult table when he came home from college. I never made it to the dining room table at my grandparent's home. I became an adult after they died.

Cousins were an important part of my life. As an only child, I played with my eight Leis cousins almost every Sunday at my grandparents'. Someone in the family was always having a birthday or a special celebration and we'd celebrate together. Photos show me and my cousins lined up on my grandparents' steps at Easter. My cousin Ed, about twelve and his brother Bob ten, are wearing leather flier's helmets with goggles pushed on top.

Ed had a collection of small books about war planes, navy ships and army insignias and a "Fight for Freedom" jigsaw puzzle. Each had an appeal to buy war bonds on back, "BUY MORE WAR BONDS. KEEP 'EM FLYING". During the war, boys memorized planes' names, their configurations and listened for the news of their involvement in battles. As a girl, I was not interested.

***

In our neighborhood, everyone sat on their front porches in warm weather after they wiped grit off the furniture. Black soot from the mill was Aliquippa's summer snow. Talking across porches became a source of neighborhood information. "Hide and Seek" would be called almost every night after dark and children would gather. With the only streetlight post as home base, anywhere on Polk Street was a hiding place. Older kids would take smaller ones to hide with them. Adults sitting in their porch chairs never told "IT" if the hidden ones crouched in their bushes, stood in shadows beside their house or straddled a branch in their tree. We were safe. "Olley, Olley, in free" or "You're IT" echoed through the neighborhood.

I grew up in a home surrounded by books and music. When we had a piano, Mother would play many kinds of music. We kept a piano when a military family was assigned to Japan, and kept my Aunt Edna's upright in between her family's moves. As a music teacher, Mother taught me basics of reading music, but I hated to practice, yet learned an appreciation for good music. When I couldn't sleep at night, I'd ask Mother to play the piano. She'd play "Barcarole" and "Taumerei".

My mother was the music teacher. At home, my dad always sang. "When You Wore a Tulip, a Big Yellow Tulip and I Wore a Big Red Rose, You Are My Sunshine, A Bicycle Built for Two" and others were his favorites. He sang when he dressed in the mornings and around the house on weekends.

My mother always had a book to read and enjoyed reading to me. I still have the Mother Goose book with nursery rhymes she read, songs she sang and handwritten notes about my favorites, "The Gingham Dog and Calico Cat" and song "Polly Put the Kettle On". She wrote, "Peggy always wants to act out the song."

Mother took me to story hour at the local library. The children's room had a stained glass window. Its many colors streaming into the room reminded me of church, so I knew the library was a special place. I'd sit with other preschoolers as the librarian read to us. My favorite book was <u>Make Way for Ducklings</u>. Later years, I spent many hours in the building reading class assigned books, <u>The Adventures of Tom Sawyer and Huckelberry Finn</u>, borrowing books for fun reading like <u>Little Women</u> and Nancy Drew mysteries, and later doing research for term papers. The BF Jones Library was a familiar place, a beautiful solid stone building with many wide steps leading up to its massive brass gates at the doors. This sanctuary sat on "the avenue" apart from the stores lining the main street. I always felt safe there.

While the war ended, I was enrolled in school for the fall of 1945. I was a big girl of five who could walk to first grade. As a year older, I would go before Carolee. "You have your own pencil and tablet," I'd tell her. "We wait outside until a bell rings to go in. The teacher reads us stories." With no kindergarten at the time and with my background, one would think I was prepared for first grade. I was not.

Hilde's and my lunchtime conversations continue.

One Tuesday after Easter, Hilde and I are eating egg salad sandwiches.

I bring out the remaining half of the family's chocolate Easter egg.

"Would you like a piece?"

Hilde shakes her head and says, "You Americans don't know how to make chocolate."

Reaching for the knife, I ask, "What do you mean?"

"Your chocolate tastes waxy", she says waving it away.

"Oh", I say cutting a piece of the solid chocolate.

"Europeans know how to make real chocolate", she says.

Hilde turns up her nose at the Easter egg as if it smells bad. "I'll bring you some real chocolate next time."

"OK", I say savoring the "waxy" chocolate.

"Mine will melt in your mouth," Hilde says nodding her head. "You won't eat American chocolate again. Have you ever eaten another country's chocolate?"

I nod. "My friend brings some back every time she visits her daughter in Switzerland."

Hilde taps her forefinger on the table three times. "Then you know what I mean."

Chapter Three

1800's-1940's
Germany

While Bruni's family lived through tragedies unification of Germany and two world wars, many of their troubles had roots in previous generations.

My grandfather Ferdinand, whom I only saw one time in my life, was a drunkard and a wife beater, even when grandmother was pregnant. She miscarried three children. Only my mother, Elisabeth(Elise) born in 1914, and my Aunt Emilie(Emily) made it into this world.

Grandfather Ferdinand's drinking was the talk of the town. Grandma was embarrassed because of the gossip he created. Ferdinand went to Elisenfels, the area where my father shot at us twenty-nine years later, the valley where lovers would go on summer nights and mothers would take their children on afternoon walks. Women and men would take a short cut in the mornings and at night to go through the valley to get back and forth to work. Everyone walked in those days. There were no cars, only horses and buggies or bicycles and motorcycles.

One morning as women and men rushed through Elisenfels on their way to work, they stopped in their tracks to look at the Volkswagen bus-size boulder sitting in the middle of the Röslau River. On top of it stood on one leg, a life-like replica of a stork with a long beak. The bird looked down at two large eggs nested beside it. It seemed to appear from nowhere. Elisenfels was an idyllic, peaceful place used as a lover's lane.

It was said that months after lovers met there, they would have a shot-gun wedding and a baby. People figured out that one night a group of men erected the stork to send that message to the population of Arzberg and surrounding villages.

Grandfather knew that women and young girls walked down the path. He would go to the little island in the middle of the river and remove his clothing. He would lie naked or stand on that island and wait for the females and expose himself. When I grew up, people would talk about it behind my back when they saw me, and school friends would tease me about my grandfather. He was arrested and put in jail. When grandmother finally lost all respect for grandfather and could not live with the shame, she divorced him.

Her parents, my great-grandparents, came from Switzerland. Grandmother's parents moved with their eight children to the western part of Germany near Nürnberg and Bayreuth, known for wonderful stage plays by Richard Wagner. Grandmother Maria Kehrer, was born in the Odenwald part of Germany.

***

The males in our family were chimney sweeps, *Schlodfeger*. They wore black leather suits, black hats, carried ladders and climbed on top of the houses in the towns to clean and build chimneys. They made very good money. We were well known because of their occupation.

When grandmother met my real Grandfather Ferdinand Neupert from München and married him, my great-grandparents gave my grandmother a very handsome dowry. They loaded a large hay wagon about the length of a house with furniture, china, silverware, pots and pans. They moved to Arzberg for him to assume the job as a forest ranger. He patrolled the area inspecting forests and wildlife. He carried a rifle and was well respected until his drinking interfered. Life should have been good for grandma when she married Ferdinand, but his drunken antics led to their divorce. After five pregnancies and abuse and embarrassment from his drinking, Grandmother divorced him.

I am not able to say when my step-grandfather Simon came into the picture, when or what year my grandmother met and married him. The first time I remember seeing him was when he came back from the war. He was gone for seven years.

Simon was in Siberia in a Russian prison camp. The treatment of the prisoners there must have been atrocious. Grandfather told me that for years he got only water and bread to eat, and I am convinced it is true. When grandfather came home he weighed only about eighty-five pounds. Although he was not tall he looked skinny and frail, almost dead. He also had a shattered shoulder. Someone hit him with a rifle and broke the shoulder. With no medical attention, it did not set right, so his shoulder was deformed and very painful.

For many years Simon was confined to the house. He had colitis and spent a lot of time in the bathroom. When he could, he managed to go to work at a china factory. His endurance is beyond my comprehension. He needed to work, would not accept disability and wanted to support my grandmother. In Simon's spare time, he stayed in bed or rested on the sofa and listened to the radio. We would find him there, when I or my brother went to their home to visit or for something to eat. Simon was always glad to see us and hugged us when we walked into their place.

Grandma and Simon lived in two rooms. They waited for years to get a larger apartment. They stayed in the kitchen/living room during the day.

Grandmother cooked and cleaned, and Grandpa Simon sat on the sofa and watched her. Once a day, he did go downstairs to a shed where he had a few cages with tamed rabbits. He would feed them and on the weekend he would kill a rabbit and skin it. Grandma cooked a rabbit on Sunday. Dinner was always delicious in Grandma's house. Although she had very little room in her kitchen, she always baked cakes and cookies too. There was always dessert after a meal.

One day a week she did all the washing on a scrubbing board and hung the clothes on the line in the backyard. Another day, she'd do the ironing on the tabletop for she had no ironing board. Every morning she would walk two kilometers down the hill to town and buy fresh meat, vegetables, fruit and goat's milk for Simon's colitis. Dinner was always ready at one o'clock in the afternoon. European people eat dinner at noon or one. For the evening meal, we would eat a salad or cold cuts or a sandwich. Every afternoon folks would have a coffee *Klatch,* cake or torte and coffee or tea. We Germans always looked forward to three o'clock. The men would also have a beer, a *Likor* or *Schnaps*. German people knew how to celebrate and have a good time.

Grandfather Simon worked in one of the china factories which had been bombarded during the war. Everyone in town and the surrounding villages worked in the Schumann factory where they produced beautiful china, practically the only source of employment in Arzberg. Originally known as *Erzberg* for the iron ore found there, the town became Arzberg in 1883. In 1887 it was known for its factories and later for Rosenthal China factories, using Thomas and Schumann and Hutchenreuther stamps. Other factories produced nails and shirts for men.

***

Grandma told me that at fifteen, my mother started dating a well-to-do farmer's boy, August. His parents had a large farm. My mom must have really liked him. They dated for three years without his parents' knowledge. Mom was pretty with her round face and very dark eyes. She had long, black, naturally curly hair. She was a little on the heavy side plump, but in those early years, men liked plump girls. German men like girls with some meat on their bones.

When Mom was eighteen-years-old she became pregnant with my sister Anneliese. When Mom had to tell August, she was very happy about the pregnancy but she had not told Grandma until she was five months along. August wanted to do the right thing for he loved my mom and wanted to marry her. They were both young and naïve. His parents had other ideas. They wanted a daughter-in-law who also came from a well to do farmer's family, not the daughter of a drunkard and divorced parents. They forbade August to see my mother. He had not told them about the baby or about my mother.

One day he walked along the Röslau River, which flows right through our town, with my unsuspecting mother. He shoved her into the water. Mother could not swim. Terribly confused and not knowing what else to do, August took off running and disappeared. Mother struggled to stay above water and started screaming. A man heard her cries for help and ran to the river to pull my mother out. He walked her home, her clothing dripping wet, exposed her swollen belly. She sneaked up the back steps of the house and got cleaned up. Grandmother still did not know about the pregnancy. The next day the rescuer came to grandmother's house and inquired about Mom's health. Grandmother told him Mom was fine. Why was he asking?

He told Grandma the whole story of how he had heard Mom's cries for help, pulled her out of the river and brought her home. The police arrested August, and he went to prison. During the war, Hitler released all the prisoners and drafted them into the *Wehrmacht* (army).

August fought the war and came home in 1946. Meanwhile in 1937, my mother had married Ludwig Maurer, my *Vater*. My brother Helmut and I were born and lived with Mom. My sister, Anneliese, lived with my grandmother. *Vater* did not want to raise August's child.

After the war, my mom was divorced from Ludwig when August came to see her. Anneliese was fourteen years old and I was five, when August begged my mom for forgiveness and asked her to marry him. My mother said to him "I can never forgive you for what you did to me and I can never marry you". So August told her that he would marry his sister-in-law, whose husband died in the war and left five children. August married his sister-in-law and raised his brother's children. He was a very good husband and father.

Faithfully, August paid child support for my sister until she was twenty-one-years old. Grandma and my mother fought over the money, because my grandmother was raising my sister Anneliese, but my mother always won.

While her early years were tragic, there was more heartache and hardship to come for my mother and my family.

29

Bruni's apartment entrance from alley between buildings on town square. She, her brother and mother lived here until Bruni was seven

Chapter Four

1860's-1940's
Germany and America

While the United States struggled with the Civil War and its aftermath, Peggy's fraternal great-grandfather Frank Joseph Leis brought his family to America from Waldmillbach in southern Germany.

Germans settled in Cincinnati, Ohio, southern Indiana, Illinois, up and down the Ohio Valley in the 1800's. The Leis family settled in Goshen, Indiana. My grandfather Charles Joseph Leis married Emma Padgett in 1901 and eventually moved his family to western Pennsylvania. In 1916, he went to Woodlawn, Pennsylvania to work in the steel mill. Woodlawn became Aliquippa, a steel making town twenty miles north of Pittsburgh.

Aliquippa was an Indian name given to a stop on the P&LE Railroad in 1880's for the Aliquippa Park, an amusement park on its route through Beaver County. In 1906 Jones&Laughlin Steel Company bought the property and built its Aliquippa Works.

Granddad Leis worked in the tin mill and later in the machine shops. He brought my grandmother, Emma Padgett Leis, to live in the brick row housing newly built for the steel workers. She wouldn't live where the plaster was still wet, the house damp, and no shade. My dad, Joseph Austin Leis, born 1905, and his sisters stayed in Indiana with relatives to finish the school year. They joined the family who had moved to better company housing on Franklin Avenue, the main street of town.

Housing was built by the mill. Workers lived in eleven of twelve plans designated by ethnic and racial groups, and position in the mill. A company store deducted the price of items bought from workers' paychecks. The town's one main street, Franklin Avenue, sat in a valley which ran from the entrance to the mill to a stone arch at the opposite end. Businesses and mill housing in numbered plans on hills lined "the avenue". Superintendents, plant foremen, and works managers lived on the three hills of Plan Six nearest to and overlooking the mill.

The Leis family eventually moved to Plan Twelve where German and Irish laborers lived. Their house was near the high school where the football announcer and noises from high school football games could be heard. The story is told that Grandma wouldn't sit on the porch when my dad played football. "I'm afraid to hear his named called for an injury," she said.

The Leis' were devout Catholics. They gathered round the radio each evening to say the rosary. Everyone knew to arrive at their house before seven to join them or after seven-thirty to not interrupt their prayers. The family attended Sunday mass regularly. I remember seeing many religious pictures around the house. Great-aunt Alice was a nun and Aunt Alice, my dad's sister, was a nun for awhile. Fascinated by a rosary plant in her bedroom window, I always wondered how its leaves knew to grow the order of rosary beads.

***

Dad worked in a man's clothing store while in high school. There he learned the art of dressing well. When he became a banker and in the public eye, he was known for being well dressed.

He graduated from Woodlawn High School in June, 1925. He took a job in the mill and rode the train to Pittsburgh to study accounting at Robert Morris Business School. He met my mother while she was teaching music in Aliquippa schools. "I won't marry anyone working in the mill," she said. Dad graduated with a degree in accounting in 1929 and took a job in a small bank in Aliquippa.

The Stock Market Crash was in October 1929. Banks were in increasing trouble. Dad told the story of how he had the responsibility of carrying the money from the Aliquippa Bank where he worked and to the larger bank in town, as people were banging on the doors of the smaller bank demanding their money. He slipped out the back door unnoticed, down an alley, and across the street, with bags full of money. People were told they could get their paychecks cashed the next day at the Woodlawn Trust Company, where J&L had their accounts. The Aliquippa Bank dissolved, and Dad was hired by the larger bank.

My maternal ancestors were Presbyterian Scots who passed through Ireland. They came to America in 1700's, before the Revolutionary War and settled in northwestern Pennsylvania in Mercer County between Pittsburgh and Erie. My Scotch-Irish grandfather, Walter Justus Craig, a farmer and small grocery store owner, met my Irish grandmother, Sarah Minerva Murphy, married and raised their family in Freedonia, Pennsylvania.

My mother, Pauline Frances Craig, was born there in 1903 the youngest of five. My grandfather died when Mother was in high school in nearby Grove City, Pennsylvania. Mother told of developing a love for music when she heard her grandfather play for barn dances. His fiddle was made of three different woods from the area. A friend of the family took Mother to Indiana to be fitted for a violin. She was known in the area as "the girl with the violin" and asked to play for various occasions.

She enrolled in Grove City College School of Music, graduated in 1925, and began her teaching career which led her to Aliquippa, where in l930's, she met my father, Austin Leis.

My mother was the original liberated woman. She graduated from college in three years and attended graduate school in New York City in the 1920's. A strict Presbyterian, she married a Catholic late in life, taught while pregnant, furnished a house before starting a family and accomplished all of this in the 1930's and early 1940's.

My parents married in November 1935 during Mother's Thanksgiving break. They were married in the parish house of my dad's family church. My Aunt Edna, mother's sister and Dad's best friend, Scotty MacDonald, were witnesses. Grandma Craig, an Irish Protestant, sat outside in the car during the ceremony. At that time, Protestants and Catholics did not participate in the other's services. It was an evening wedding, so it must have been dark and cold in

November. I think it is sad that Grandma Craig could or would not see her youngest daughter marry.

Following the wedding, my paternal grandparents held a reception at their house for their only son and his new wife. Mother became the second Pauline Leis as my Great-grandfather Leis had named his daughter Pauline. Granddad Leis asked my mother if she would ever convert to Catholicism, and when she answered "No", he said that no one else in the family would ever ask her again. She continued to be a Presbyterian and my dad a Catholic, both active in their churches. With Mother's example of a woman strong in her faith, I became strong in mine.

I was baptized Catholic and went to Mother's church with her until I started school. She had to sign an agreement when she and Dad were married that their children would be baptized and raised Catholic.

I grew up listening to Mother and Grandma Craig singing Protestant hymns. When I attended their church in my preschool years, I would sit with someone in the congregation while Mother directed the choir. My doll, Suzie Q, sat with me. She had wooden legs and arms, and I remember being scolded when her legs banged on the wooden pews during a service. When I started school, I attended Catholic Sunday school and church.

Most Sundays, my dad and I would go Grandma and Granddad Leis' after ten o'clock mass. Mother went to her church where she was choir director and taught organ lessons after services. My grandparents, in German tradition, would serve a pot roast dinner at one o'clock. "Will you stay today?" Grandma would ask. And each Sunday, my dad and I would say "No" and leave to go home for a light lunch with Mother. The three of us had our Sunday meal in the dining room at six o'clock.

Mother's sister Aunt Edna, her husband Uncle Paul, and their twins, Patty and Paul, eight years older than me came one Sunday a month. The four of them drove the hour in from Wilkinsburg, outside of Pittsburgh. On our way home from Grandma and Granddad's, my dad and I would play a game, "Would their car be in front of our house or not?" We would have an afternoon and a meal together and they would leave. Another Sunday we would drive to their house for the same. We did not leave until the end of the radio show "The Shadow" or "Mr.&Mrs North".

***

Mother and Dad had a group of local friends who loved to play cards. They would rotate hosting Saturday nights. When all were at our house, I would lie upstairs in bed and hear them screaming and laughing. I remember thinking "Nothing could be that funny!" After awhile I could identify each person by his/her laugh. My mother was a serious person. My dad brought humor to her life. I heard later that on those evenings, Mother could be very funny.

Summer vacations were annually spent at Lake Erie shores. For one week, Mother, Dad and I, Aunt Edna and Uncle Paul rented a cottage within walking distance of the lake. I remember nights sitting around bonfires on the beach, sleeping out on screened-in porches feeling secure surrounded by the night and the sound of waves lapping on shore. I learned to swim on my mother's back. One time, I went completely underwater and still recall the panic of swallowing water, madly struggling to surface, and relief at seeing my parents reaching for me. One year, several families from Polk Street rented cottages near each other. There are photos of Carolee, her sister DJ and me wearing white bathing caps floating in inner tubes. On the beach, our mothers unpacked sandwiches onto blankets under beach umbrellas. We would spend whole days in the sun. It was fun to see Carolee's dad, a policeman, and Joe the milkman, out of uniform and my parents in bathing suits.

The War was over the summer of '45 and it was time for me to start school.

One day at lunch, Hilde brings a porcelain figurine to the table. "I saw this on the mantle. Where did you get this bird?" she asks.

"A former neighbor gave it to me," I say.

"You know it's a Goebel," she says turning over the sulphur crested Cockatoo perched on a branch.

"No, is it special?"

"It certainly is," she says. "See here 'made in West Germany'". Hilde strokes the bird. "Who is this person?"

"She lived in our old neighborhood and always struck up a conversation when I passed her house taking my babies for a walk."

"Is she German?"

I nodded. "She spoke with an accent like yours."

"Well, she must have liked you a lot. Do you have others?"

"I have three Hummels."

I show her the small porcelain chimney sweep. "I bought him in Germany."

She picks up the Nativity Virgin. "And where did you get this?"

"My neighbor Alice gave it to me."

"And this one?" Hilde picks up the girl holding a flower.

"My friend, Margie, gave her to me."

Hilde turns over each one and sees the stamp. "Yep, they're all German."

Chapter Five

1945-1959
Marktredwitz and Arzberg

While Germany surrendered May 7, 1945, the next day May 8, 1945 VE Day, the war officially ended in Europe, school days soon started for Bruni.

When it was time for me to enroll in grade school, Mom had a pretty dress made for me and bought shoes and a *Zuckertüte*. It is the custom in Germany to carry this large ice cream cone shape about two-and-a-half feet long. The inside is colorful, lined with pretty fabric. On the first day of school little girls and boys proudly carry one of these Zuckertüte to school, usually stuffed full of candies and small toys. "Where are your candies?" they asked, "Where are your toys?" We had no money for toys or candy. I hugged mine close to my body. It held only small apples.

I liked school and I made pretty good grades. One day when I was in second grade my mom called Helmut and me together and said, "We are moving back to Arzberg. I do not feel safe here in Marktredwitz because your *Vater* is harassing and following us." Arzberg is about twelve kilometers down the road and five kilometers from Tschechoslovakia.

I liked *Oma's* town because I remembered when we lived with her. We had gone to the train station to meet Aunt Emilie and Uncle Paul from there. Memories of the bomb raid and the burning boy came back to me. Mom said "I waited for several years for a reply from Arzberg city hall for an available apartment. We were on a waiting list to acquire an apartment. Now one is available."

We got a one bedroom apartment, kitchen with living room combined, the bathroom was outside in the backyard. It was a barracks with three outhouses all the neighbors used. It was very primitive. The government rule was that when I got older I could no longer sleep in the same bed or room with my brother, so the city gave me a bedroom located downstairs. It had a separate entrance.

I did not like the school there. Everyone knew that I was the daughter of Elisabeth Maurer, a divorcee and the granddaughter of Maria Neubert also a divorcee. There were rumors about Ferdinand Neubert, my grandfather. Even the teachers treated my brother and me differently because of our relatives. The boys followed me home and kept calling me, "*Schlotfegerl*" little chimney sweep, because my male relatives cleaned chimneys for a living. We had no money to purchase clothes or books for school and I missed a lot of school because of no food or clean clothes. I could never participate in art because I had no materials. The school would not provide these things, the parents were responsible to supply them. Some schools were closed because of the bombings.

My school was a public school in a Lutheran country. It had Lutheran and Catholic students. The priest came twice a week and taught religion to the Lutheran class. We started every day with a prayer. If we gave a wrong answer in school, one teacher slapped our ears with a flat hand or a ruler. We were not allowed to write left-handed. Those who did were forced to write with their right hand.

All the children lined up in the schoolyard daily to receive free lunches. The *Amerikans* had come to Germany in 1945 and it was decided that the *Amerikan Armee* would provide food for all the children. It was wonderful, but we didn't like pea soup or tomato soup with noodles. We had to bring a kettle or pitcher from home. Someone would fill up the pitcher and we had to eat it all. A guard was stationed at the gate. No one was going home until the soup was gone.

We would play in the schoolyard after school and kill time, all to no avail. Finally we gulped down the cold soup and went to the gate to go home. We also received Lifesavers and Hershey chocolate with almonds. We loved that. I would only eat a few Lifesavers at a time and keep the rest for later.

After the war, we had plenty of money but we could not buy anything. The stores were empty. There was no merchandise because of inflation and ruination of the DM (*Deutsche Mark*). Most of Germany was destroyed and could not produce anything. Mom found a salesman who sold herring. One herring was five DM, which would be about three dollars right now in *Amerikan* currency. With cooked potatoes, we ate pickled herring for supper every day.

One day someone spread the word that in a booth down on the corner, a man was selling horsemeat, sausage, salami and wieners. We bought him out. He came every Saturday. We often wondered if what he sold was horsemeat, but we didn't question it. It was a matter of survival.

Several times my mother would save money for shoes for my brother. When Helmut was about fifteen, he got a new pair of shoes. He put them on and went outside to talk to his friends. He didn't come home until late in the evening. His new shoes were totally ruined. The soles were hanging from the shoes. Because of the war, they were made of cheap materials.

Helmut had gone behind the house where there was a long field and played soccer with his friends. Mother was mad, but she couldn't bring herself to hit him. Wadek got a very thick belt which he used to sharpen his razor and beat Helmut for the longest time. It was horrible. Mother sat in the corner by the stove and didn't do a thing to intervene.

When she was healthy, Mom got a job in the china factory, leaving my brother and me home alone after school. My grandmother lived a few blocks away still at the same place she lived when we stayed with her and my mother was in the concentration camp. Aunt Emilie lived around the corner so we stayed there sometimes when Mom and Wadek were at work.

One evening Helmut and I played with a chair by the window. We saw Mom coming home from work. My brother was pushing me and suddenly the chair seat gave way and broke in the middle. My leg stuck between the wood and the seat. I tried to pull my leg out. In the process, a nail ripped through my skin. I felt terrible pain shooting through my leg. As I pulled my leg free I saw a gaping hole in my flesh. It was about three inches long and a half-inch deep.

As soon as Mom came in the door, she knew something had happened. Helmut and I were both screaming. The same evening she took me down the street to a doctor. He had no medicine to apply to the wound, so he put baby powder on it and bandaged the leg. After two weeks the wound had not healed and got infected. I was limping around and the leg was hurting me badly.

Not too far from my house on the *Rathausstr Nr. 5* there was a large store. When the *Amerikan Armee* came to town, the Germans vacated this store and a small *Armee* post was created. This post was to patrol the border which was only five kilometers away. We had to pass the *Armee* post to get to the stores and the train station. We walked over the bridge where the river ran through the town. When I had the injury to my leg, I was limping past the *Armee Post* to purchase some groceries. My brother and I did all the shopping for some days my mom would never leave the house.

Usually there were *Armee* jeeps and trucks parked alongside the building. *Amerikan* soldiers sat on the steps or played a little baseball. Soldiers would go in and come out. They hollered or talked in a funny language. I couldn't understand a word.

I often noticed a short fellow with black hair and a white uniform. I figured he was a doctor. I was only eight-years-old and concentrating on limping to the store. As I passed the building and the soldiers, I noticed out of the corner of my eye that someone was behind me. Suddenly I was lifted up. I felt arms around me. Someone was carrying me towards this building.

The soldiers stopped playing ball and watched as this man in the white uniform rushed passed them and disappeared with me inside the building. I found myself sitting on top of a table. With a grin, the man lifted my leg toward him and started to take the dirty bandage off. He was angry at the looks of the wound. It looked nasty. He proceeded to clean the wound with some red liquid and it burned like hell. I cried out in pain. The doctor comforted me and wrapped clean bandages around my leg.

Every once in a while he looked at me and smiled. A nametag on his shirt said "Chico". He handed me some gum and I did not know what it was. He also gave me some German money, then lifted me to the floor, led me to the door and out to the sidewalk. I turned left and headed for the store. He did say something but I could not understand what he said. I made up my mind that I would not walk past that building again for it was very painful when Chico applied that red stuff. Later, I found out that it was iodine. He applied it directly to my leg and it burned horribly.

A teacher at school scolded me for associating with *Amerikans* and called me an *Amerikan* lover. America had been our enemy. About a week later I, again, made my way past the building and made sure Chico was not sitting on the steps. I almost was passed the building and almost forgot about the soldier when suddenly coming from nowhere he scooped me up again and carried me toward the building.

He knew I was avoiding him and he was waiting for me. He repeated the same procedure and applied a new bandage. This time he gave me some chocolate and talked in a peculiar language which I thought sounded corny. As my leg was healing, Chico and I became friends. Whenever I passed his *Armee Post* he would stop and talk to me or put his arm around my shoulder. I finally felt how it must feel to have a father.

Several months passed and I would see Chico often. Once he gave me a German songbook. I do not know where he got it. I was so happy. I told my mom about him the first time he changed my bandage.

One day after I came home from school, I looked up the street and saw *Armee* trucks, jeeps and tanks lined up in front of the *Armee Post*. I walked towards the building and all the vehicles. The soldiers were already seated in the vehicles. I could not comprehend what that meant. Chico was sitting behind the wheel of a jeep and he smiled at me and took my hand and held it. He looked sad and he tried to tell me something. I did not know what he tried to tell me. The vehicles started up and moved slowly away from the curb. Chico let go of my tiny hand and started his jeep. With his back in view, he turned and gave me one last smile. Soon he was out of sight and all the vehicles drove down the street and disappeared.

I could not believe they were gone. I slowly realized that they were going forever and I would never see him again. Sobbing, I ran home and went up the stairs to tell my mom about Chico's departure. I threw myself into my mother's arms and I cried and cried. The next day a new group of soldiers arrived to patrol the border. I found out that every four months new troops would arrive. The old one would leave and be stationed elsewhere. I would never forget Chico and his kindness to me.

For the first time in my life, I loved a male beside my brother and my step-grandfather Simon, with whom I had a very special bond.

***

Our church and school were only one-half kilometers up the hill from the *Armee Post*. It was surrounded by a very high wall. If you would go up to the church tower you could see right into the country called "*Tscheslovakia*". The *Tscheks* would patrol the border on one side and the *Amerikans* would march up and down on the other side. Anyone who would cross the border, civilians or soldiers would be shot immediately. When the border was erected citizens were very distraught for they were separated from their loved ones. Relatives would not see each other for forty years.

Before the war, my mom and brother and I would ride on the train into *Tscheslovakia* to a town called Eger. We would take a coach at the train station and ride into town. Horses and buggies would travel down the streets. We would visit my grandmother's sister and go shopping. They had handmade things for sale and the workmanship was wonderful. It was a beautiful country with tree-filled parks and cobblestone streets, magnificent churches and exquisite cafes and restaurants. After the war, a border was erected. The Soviets and eventually Communists took over. The train could only go to the border and then turn around and come back. Many people fled to Germany right before the border was erected. They came from the Sudetenland. It was devastating for people being torn apart from their relatives.

Germans were forced to take people in and rent them space, for the country was overpopulated and no housing was available. My Aunt Emilie took in a man from East Germany named Schäfer. I do not remember his first name. Everyone called him by the last name. He was a blond, about forty years old. My mother's girlfriend came often to visit because she liked Schäfer.

Everyone seemed to like him. Emilie's children (two girls and three boys) liked Schäfer, too and he played with them and watched them when Emilie and Uncle Paul worked. He would take the children to the woods to pick berries. One Easter he took them and other neighbor children on a long walk. I went along also.

I observed that Schäfer paid a lot of attention to my cousin Ingrid. She is a year older than me and she must have been ten-years-old then. One time they went on a hike in the woods and when they came home Ingrid's dress was full of blueberry stains at the backside. Aunt Emilie asked Ingrid what happened and Schäfer said "Oh, she fell backwards into the blueberry bushes". Emilie did not bother to imagine any farther.

For three years, Ingrid and I played together. In front of the house we would play Hopscotch, Hide-and-Go-Seek and jump rope with other children. We would talk when we went on walks. Ingrid was a fat kid and she had trouble with her eyes and she had to wear thick glasses because she was born cross-eyed. She turned out to be fat like Aunt Emilie. Uncle Paul was very skinny.

One day Ingrid and I talked, and she said that Schäfer was doing things to her and I said "What things?" Ingrid said, "Well, he comes into my room at night and gets into my bed, he puts a stick between my legs". I asked her "What stick?" Ingrid said, "He puts something wet on that stick and he puts it between my legs. It really hurts." I didn't know what to think of it, because I never heard of anything like that. We were so naïve. We were not allowed to talk about sex or ask about where children came from.

My mother would slap me if I brought up the subject, no one told us anything about the facts of life, not even in school. So I was going around telling other kids about what Schäfer was doing to Ingrid and soon every kid talked about it.

One day I was in the backyard picking wild flowers in the field where my brother played soccer. I heard someone calling for me and when I turned around, it was Helmut. He said, "Boy, are you in trouble. Mom wants to talk to you. You're going to get it for what you said about Schäfer and Ingrid."

My heart sank and I was scared to death about what was going to happen. I was afraid of my mother. The last few years she turned to beating me for every little thing. There were times when she lost her temper and would beat me with her hands, then the belt and beat me to the floor and kick me. Those were the times when I lost all joy in life and wanted to run away or kill myself. I could not understand what happened to my sweet and gentle mother from a long time ago.

I hung around the field for hours. It became evening and the sun started going down. I was getting hungry, but no way was I going home. I went over and sat on the railing of a fence and kept looking towards the house. Soon it was dark and the lights came on in the windows of all the houses. Even the storks nestled on top of chimneys got ready to sleep. It started to get chilly and I started freezing. Finally I thought, well if Mom wants to beat me, so be it. I'm going home and tell what Ingrid told me.

I went across the yard and went into the house and up the stairs and went in. There was Mom, Aunt Emilie, Uncle Paul and Ingrid, Wadek and Helmut. I expected the worst. I almost urinated into my pants I was so scared. Immediately I started sobbing. I was tired and hungry for I hadn't eaten since lunchtime. I wanted to go to bed and hide under the covers.

When Aunt Emilie saw me she came up to me and took my hands. She told me to sit beside her and tell her what I had been telling the children in the neighborhood. I repeated everything. I could not believe it when Emilie hugged me and told me not to be afraid. I know my mother would have smacked me left and right, but Emilie was different. She never had a difficult life and so she had a better disposition than my mom. My mother was bitter and often let her anger and frustration out on me.

Emilie explained that they confronted Schäfer and he denied it and decided to leave. Ingrid stuck to her story and Paul and Emilie took Ingrid to the doctor the next day. The doctor confirmed that Ingrid had been raped for months.

Schäfer was investigated and arrested. There was a family in the small village past the valley where my father was shooting at us. Schäfer confessed he went to the village often to visit those friends. They had a daughter about eleven or twelve. In winter he would take this little girl ice-skating on the river where my mother almost drowned about twenty years before. Schäfer forced this little girl onto the ice and raped her. Both stories proved true and he went to trial, got convicted and went to prison for seven years. Then we knew why he wasn't interested in my mother's friend. He liked little girls!

I guess I was a heroine for awhile. Because of me and my "Big Blabbermouth" it all came out. Aunt Emilie was always very nice to me afterwards. When she and Uncle Paul moved to another place out to the country, they let me come and stay with them for weeks at a time during summer vacation. I always ate good food there.

***

At thirteen or fourteen, I went to movies all day Sundays seeing the actor Audie Murphy, the movies "Hunchback of Notre Dame" and "Gone With the Wind" in German. We had no money for full price. We went in for spare change after the movies started. Over and over I sang Elvis Presley's "Don't Be Cruel".

When I graduated from grade school at fourteen, I had Konfirmation. Our family was Lutheran as were most of the families in the region. We didn't have much money but my mother and grandma did their best. Grandmother Maria was my godmother and she bought me a dress and shoes. I had a perm and I looked nice, small and skinny. Mom bought one half of a cow and we had all the meat smoked. We cooked for days and invited a few people to celebrate with us.

While Germany and its people were still recovering from the war, I struggled through my teen-age-years and got ready to find a job.

12/29/2010

Peggy's home on Polk Street. She lived here with her parents until she went to college, returning for two years when teaching before marriage

Chapter Six

1945-1954
Aliquippa, Pennsylvania

While the Pacific phase of WWII ended and a formal document of surrender signed, Peggy started school in the United States.

I crouched under a bench in the garage the second day of school. "I don't want to go back." I wailed to my mother when she found me. "My teacher is too big!" Mrs. Henry was the largest woman I had ever seen. I was afraid of her. My mother walked me back to school spanking me with each step. Yet I have fond memories of Mrs. Henry. During terrible thunder storms that year she read stories to us and waited to dismiss us until the storms ended. From her, I learned to read with Dick and Jane. Sundays, I practiced at home lying on my stomach in front of the console radio following the words in the comic section with "Puck, The Radio Reader".

Everyone walked to and from New Sheffield School and home for lunch. I walked down to the end of Polk Street to a path down a hillside, crossed a bridge and trudged up another hill. Five or six children, whose mothers worked, ate their sack lunches in the teachers' lounge every day. When my mother had an all day meeting, she packed me a lunch. It was a treat to eat a sack lunch with them. Sometimes, I walked to our neighbor Mary Dyer's home for lunch. Smiling, she always served tomato soup and grilled cheese sandwiches. Her daughter, Lois, was in high school and gone all day. I think Mary Dyer enjoyed having company in the middle of her day.

At school I bought stamps for war bonds from my allowance. Each child had a stamp book to fill. I pasted in my stamps every week, happy to be doing my part. A full book bought a war bond to help pay for war expenses.

One time while walking down the hill from school, I fell forward onto the stones we called bone coal. With gravel in my knee and blood pouring down my leg, I limped home. Because Carolee's dad was a policeman and knew First Aid, he plucked the stones out of my knee with tweezers, washed and applied a stinging, smelly, brown salve, then wrapped up my leg. Sitting in their upstairs bathroom where he treated me, I could look out and see the hill where I fell. I knew I had to walk up and down that nasty hill the rest of my days at that school. A year afterward the city erected a series of open steel steps with multiple landings leading to the school. Boys thought it was funny to stand under the steps and embarrass girls saying they'd seen their underpants.

Before descending the steps from school to home, I had a ritual. Standing at the top I'd look over the treetops and the valley below to find my house at the top of the next hill. Our white two story clapboard stood out from the other houses. I could see the bedroom window where Grandma Craig watched for me. I'd look to the right for my Aunt Ola's house on Tyler Street. I felt safe, my family waited for me on the next hill. "Can you really see me?" I'd ask my grandma. She'd smile and nod.

Some mornings, Carolee and I would ride in the milk truck with our neighbor, Joe, the milkman. He drove us from Polk Street down the alley to the next street. Then we would take Tyler Street steps, down the hill, cross the bridge and climb steps up the hill to school. We felt important. We had a ride!

Other times I met girls coming from across Grand Ave. and walked with them. One of the girls told me she had just become an aunt. "How could she be an aunt?" I asked my mother. My aunts were older and I thought everybody's aunts should be older. My mother had to draw a family tree to finally make sense to me that a young person could be an aunt.

In first grade I met a lifelong friend, Lynn. Her mother was a teacher also. Lynn and I spent many hours together at her house and mine. Her mother baked brownies that tasted like none other! Lynn and I were chosen one year to be angels at the school Christmas play. A photo shows us unsmiling in our white robes and tinsel haloes standing guard at the sides of a Nativity scene, me with shoulder length dark brown curls and Lynn in long honey-colored braids. We joke about being type-cast. We didn't see ourselves as angels!

New Sheffield School sat across from an open area called Fireman's Field. Every spring the circus came to that field. A parade advertised its entrance through our town and into our lives. From our classroom windows we could watch the elephants pulling the wagons and helping set up the huge tent. Men and women scurried about establishing a little city while animals prowled and roared in their cages. Our excitement carried over into our homes as we begged our families to take us to the evening shows. There we ate spun sugar cotton candy and popcorn and "oohed and awed" at the live acts.

During the last part of my first grade, I had measles and ear surgery, not an uncommon result. Mother said I was delirious with the pain from the earache. Lying in my parent's bed, I heard Mother downstairs making arrangements to take me to the hospital. I had no idea what was to happen. There, I was scheduled for surgery. I screamed at being taken away from my mother and tied down on a hard table. Terrified, I struggled to free myself as a mask was clamped on my face. Smelling ether, I fell asleep. If the procedure had been explained to me, I don't think I would have been uncooperative.

After Sunday school classes, in second grade I made my First Communion. I wore a white store bought dress, my payment for modeling in a fashion show. My mother made my shoulder length veil and white headpiece. I carried a small prayer book and crystal rosary. Covered water fountains in the school halls kept us from drinking the hour before Communion.

In photos with Grandma Leis, at her house, I stand in my Communion dress with her standing in her freshly starched apron and flowered house dress. Back home, my parents and friends posed with me under the rose arbor in our side yard. My godmother, Aunt Rene gave me a statue of St. Theresa. I felt special surrounded by family and friends passing another milestone.

In elementary school years, Margey joined Carolee and me as a neighborhood playmate. Margey was Jewish, and I enjoyed going to her huge house. Her father, Morris, could always be found in the living room smoking a cigar and reading the newspaper away from the hustle and bustle of the household. Her mother, Edith, always in the kitchen, introduced me to matzoh and homemade chicken soup. Margey's teenage brother had a huge collection of "Archie" comic books which I spent hours reading at home on his one day lending policy.

Carolee, Margey and I played with doll furniture under our dining room table. We consolidated our miniature furniture and our names to make Hotel CalPeMar. The three of us spent hours arranging and rearranging the furniture into bedrooms, kitchen, and lobbies and speaking for our "guests".

I joined Girl Scouts of America. To earn botany and communication badges, I grew a begonia plant from a cutting and went with the troop to a radio station for a live Saturday morning broadcast at KDKA studios in Pittsburgh. The begonia thrived on our front porch and watching the radio program in progress was exciting. I saw the people whose voices I had listened to at home.

Summers, Lynn and I went to Girl Scout day camps, then overnight camps. One summer, we volunteered for latrine duty, not knowing what it was. Everyone in camp knew our task. We smelled like Lysol the whole week! I was proud to wear the uniform. Being part of a big organization was important to me, and I tried to be a good scout, although I lost an award for our camp cabin by fainting on the last leg of a five mile hike. Scouting lasted until junior high years when members of our troop scattered and school activities entered my life.

My sixth grade teacher is one I will never forget. Miss Mellot had no children of her own but knew children. She was strict and prepared us well for moving on from New Sheffield School. Most of us had been classmates from first grade. We were excited to be going downtown to another school.

In that year, 1950 during the Korean War, we had our first school air raid drill. We were to run home and have our parents call back our arrival times. Petrified, I sprinted home thinking we were being bombed and Aliquippa would be destroyed and leveled like the towns in Germany I'd seen on newsreels.

During my elementary school years, my dad had a heart attack. It was a scary time. My dad was rarely sick. My serious, formal mother suffered migraines and I was used to her "taking to her bed", but now my funny, playful father was in pain. He spent time in the hospital. Back home, he was to remain on one floor. The dining room table was carried upstairs into my bedroom, and my bed moved downstairs in its place. I was confused. "Why didn't the hospital fix him?" I asked my mother. "I was OK after my surgery. Why is he so weak?"

We bought the first television in the neighborhood to keep him company. Dad always said we never knew if friends and family came to visit him or to see the "newfangled thing".

That Christmas he sat in a chair and coached me in setting up his Lionel train display around the Christmas tree. I wired the tracks, transformers and the lighting for inside the little village buildings. Dad trusted me to run the trains, his treasures bought the first year he and Mother were married. I felt grown up and proud that I could help keep Christmas the same for us during his recovery.

***

Family celebrations always included a game of Tripoli. Granddad carried a sock full of pennies with a clasp on top like a purse which he jingled until the grown-ups agreed to a game.

At one of the family parties at our house, I decided to play a trick on my dad. At school I had seen it done and everyone laughed. When my dad leaned over the table to make a play on the Tripoli board, I pulled his chair out from under him. When he crouched to sit back down, he fell to the floor. Everyone gasped and looked at me. Mother sent me to my room. As others helped him up, Dad shook off the incident saying he wasn't hurt. I sneaked out onto the porch. Ashamed to be seen, I hid in the dark on the glider. One of my older cousins sitting there just looked at me. We didn't speak. Sometime later my dad began leaning to one side as he stood and surgery was recommended.

Mother called many doctors for recommendations for a good back surgeon and found one in Pittsburgh twenty miles away. I was frantic as my dad was driven away. Would he be as scared as I was when I had surgery? I wanted to go with him and tell him what would happen. I don't know if my trick had caused Dad's back surgery. I never had the nerve to ask

For protection while he was gone, my mother bought a dog, a white fox terrier with black and brown spots. Mother taught Spot to bark at men. Spot learned her lesson well. She barked daily at the mailman, the milkman, the cleaner deliveryman and my dad. When he returned home from the hospital, Spot wouldn't let him in the house! Dad picked up the dog by the scruff of the neck and looked her right in the eyes and said, "This is MY house" and dropped her onto the floor. Spot never barked at Dad again, but growled every time he came near

Evenings when my dad came home from work, he would find Carolee and me huddled together at the end of the couch watching the cowboy show "Hopalong Cassidy" on television. Dad would come around the corner and scare us by yelling, "BANG". We heard his car come in the driveway, knew he was coming and always jumped as if we'd been shot. Dad was also known for drawing stick figure cartoons of what was happening around us. Carolee and I would sit on each side of him in a chair and giggle as he drew frames of figures adding words in balloons exactly as said. He drew in his receding hairline, Mother's glasses and spots on our dog.

For my tenth birthday my parents bought me girl and boy twin dolls. My mother and aunts sewed and knitted them blue and pink matching outfits. There is a photo of my aunts, uncles and cousins surrounding my grandma and granddad with me standing directly behind them holding the two dolls. Granddad is holding his hat, so Tripoli must have been played after ice cream and cake.

In the meantime, Carolee had moved to another neighborhood in Aliquippa. We remained friends and spent time together on weekends and on the phone.

***

A new neighbor entered my life. Joyce moved in across the street. She was a few years younger than I, a slender blonde with a wide smile. We became fast friends and practically lived at each other's houses.

Her Ukrainian family introduced me to another world. One time I ran home calling to my mom, "Do you know they make noodles on their dining room table?" I had never seen noodles outside of plastic packages! Another time calling, "Her family eats sauerkraut ON their hot dogs!" Her aunts spoke in a foreign tongue to her *Babba*, Grandmother. Joyce, and her younger brother Joe, and I spent many summer afternoons playing cards or day-long games of Monopoly. I was learning to play the clarinet and Joyce the accordion. We both hated practicing and eventually gave up playing the instruments. When in high school, I joined a chorus and she became a cheerleader.

The boy on the far side of the duplex next door did practice his music. Every evening the neighborhood heard him playing his bassoon from the open window in his third floor bedroom. As a result, I can always identify a bassoon's tones in an orchestra.

His older sister married a man in the United States Air Force. At twelve, I babysat for their two boys when she and her boys lived next door with her parents. One time I was interviewed by two Air Force officers about her husband. I was no help as I never saw the man. He was always away on duty. Being questioned by two men in uniform on my front porch was intimidating. Mother sat with me. My information was truthful, but sketchy.

Saturday mornings were spent with my neighbor, Lois, who lived down the street. A tall redhead, she was older than I. We played paper dolls and listened to Kipling's Jungle Book stories on the radio. When she started dating, she and her boyfriend would give me a ride in his car up the hill to my house as they left on a date. I thought I was special to be that part of her life, too. In later years, I would ride to and from Pittsburgh with her parents on Sunday nights when they drove Lois back to nursing school.

***

Before I went to junior high school, I was given "The Talk" by my mother. She sat in a high-back living room chair and I perched on the arm of the couch facing her. Mother spoke in her schoolteacher voice giving me the facts of life. I heard it as a lecture. When she asked if I had any questions, I asked why she and Dad had no more children. She took a deep breath and said, "I was pregnant with another child when you were three," she paused. "I tripped over an electric chord while chasing a cat off the furniture." She whispered. "I lost the baby."

I was shocked! I had never heard that I might have had a sibling. I spent days speculating what my life could have been as a sister. Would we look alike? What would her name be? Maybe I would have a brother! I had stopped the Leis name by being a girl. He would carry on the family name. Was my dad disappointed? My father had a brother who died in childhood and my dad became the carrier of the name. Was the whole Leis family disappointed that I was a girl? No one voiced their opinion, but I felt guilty. I never mentioned this to my family.

Then I asked Mother about her body cast. I knew she wore one when I was a baby, but I didn't know why. "When I was teaching music and pregnant with you, I moved a piano and injured my back," she said looking beyond me as if seeing the scene again. "Doctors agreed not to operate until after I recovered from your birth. I wore a full body cast."

"Who took care of me?" I asked trying to figure this all out.

Then she told me that they'd hired a daytime nurse named Catherine to take care of me my first two years.

A few weeks later while crawling around in the attic, I found the cast. The heavy plaster tube with tattered jersey-like covering had imprisoned my mother for a long time. I sat and stared at it, saddened that by wearing it my mother must have been miserable as well as disappointed that she couldn't pick up her little girl.

For the rest of her life, Mother wore a laced corset with metal staves and corrective shoes for support. We made annual sojourns into Pittsburgh to a special store for her to be measured for a new corset.

***

In junior high school I met students from all five elementary schools in Aliquippa. There Lynn and I met Elaine. We were as different as our hairstyles. Elaine had short, dark naturally curly hair. Lynn had bangs and a page boy. As my hair grew longer it hung in a ponytail enhanced by my mother's switch, a hairpiece she had once used for braids. It matched my hair perfectly. Mother's hair was snow white by that time.

Lynn, Elaine and I had different homerooms and classes, but met everyday for lunch and participated in intramural sports. I wasn't athletically inclined, so I volunteered to referee after-school basketball and volleyball games.

We took public busses to and from Franklin Junior High and walked half way up a hill to school. Two years later, we would walk further up the hill to high school. To catch a bus home, we would walk to the bottom of the hill, or downtown. I was not allowed to catch a public bus any lower on "the avenue" than three-fourths of the way down, at the company store. The mill workers got on first at the mouth of the mill and deserved the seats. Students boarded at stops further up the avenue and filled the bus. Mill men held our books while we stood holding onto straps, hot, tired and swaying with the bus' movements and trying not to fall in the men's laps.

Catching the public bus in the morning was an art. The bus would make its way up the Terrace unloading men from the night shift, then work its way down the hill picking up students. At Polk Street, I could get a seat only when I was first at the stop. Six of us would get on the bus slowly allowing more time for Joyce. She always came running out of her house with one hand in her coat sleeve holding up a doughnut, the other holding her books, yelling "Wait for me!" This routine continued for the next four years.

***

As a teen I was allowed to go to the movies with a friend. My girlfriends and I sat watching movies starring Esther Williams and Doris Day, picking out the clothes the actresses wore and claiming them as our own. My favorite movie was "Magnificent Obsession" with Jane Wyman and Rock Hudson. I collected movie star cards and Hollywood dolls, miniature dolls dressed in theme clothes which lined the bookshelves in my room.

Although my mother was Protestant, she was the one who quizzed me each week on my Baltimore Catechism questions and answers in preparation for Sunday school. I attended every Sunday before mass for eight years until Confirmation. A paper cross with stars on it for my correctly answered questions sat on our mantel. I think my mother was as proud of it as I. She would come to mass with my dad and me on Christmas and Easter and special occasions. My Catholic dad never stepped foot in her Presbyterian church.

In eighth grade I was confirmed in the Catholic faith. Saturday morning classes with Sister Lucien prepared me for the sacrament. A patient nun, she answered every question we students had about faith, boys and growing up. I felt prepared, yet my Confirmation day was spoiled. Wearing a new dress and knowing a party would follow, I was happy going into church, and left in tears. I was shocked to be slapped hard by the Bishop, a reminder that I was a soldier of Christ! I was not expecting such a strong reminder! My face stung, my eyes teared. I stumbled up from kneeling in front of him. I sulked for the rest of the day. My new dress, friends and celebration didn't mean much anymore. I felt sorry for myself, and Mother scolded me for my sullen behavior.

Junior high school (seventh and eighth grades) was difficult. I had classes with teachers my mom had taught with and my dad was on the school board. I felt as if the whole school staff was watching me. And they were! My mom knew how I was doing in classes before I got home. I did not make the best grades. Lynn and Elaine were my mainstays.

We talked a lot before and after school. I think that was when my parents bought an upstairs phone. My dad could never understand how girls had so much to talk about after they'd seen each other all day. We became interested in boys at the same time and developed silent crushes on certain boys, followed their movements, wrote in our diaries and whispered about them, but never dated them.

Lynn, Elaine and I were part of a group called "Pushers and Sweepers", our first leadership roles in junior high. Students went home for lunch or ate brown bag lunches in certain classrooms. We were in charge of assigning pushers to push desks to one side of room after lunch so sweepers could sweep the classroom. Pushers lined up the desks again for the next class. These years were our first with hall monitors who directed hall traffic. To this day I remember to walk to the right as directed then! Monitors requested hall passes when one was out of a room during class. These were my first days of rules to be observed for order among many students in a large building, getting me ready for a more crowded high school.

***

Summers I spent a week on my Aunt Clara and Uncle Joe's farm. I picked berries and potatoes on hot days with my cousins, watched my aunts making apple butter in the summer kitchen off the main kitchen, went to town for shopping Friday nights, and drove back Sundays for church. Sunday afternoons we would look forward to Aunt Ola and Cousin Bob's visit. It was lonely on the farm when the only people we saw all week were each other and the animals. The cow path went past the living room window, and it was not unusual to see a cow's face peering in at us, at times looking as lonely as I felt.

While the Korean stalemate was ending, it was time to catch the same local busses and walk further up the hill, cross the street and up another hill for new adventures and high school years.

One October lunchtime, Hilde says, "You know I win a lot of Halloween costume contests at the Germania club and Männerchor. What do you think I can be this year?"

I'd seen photos of her in various costumes and knew why she won prizes.

Hilde giggles. "I've been a barmaid, a bag lady, the Statue of Liberty and a pioneer woman. No one guesses who I am. I fool them every time."

"Well, right now there's a commercial on TV where the ape jumps on a suitcase to prove its durability," I say.

She thinks for a minute. "And no one would know who I am completely covered with a gorilla suit."

I nod. "We have a hard suitcase in the attic you could use."

Hilde leans towards me. "Have you ever dressed up as an adult?"

I nod. "For Lit Club we dress up as literary characters. I've been Shakespeare, a tree from <u>A Tree Grows in Brooklyn</u>, and Scheherazade."

"And what else?"

"For Murder Mystery Nights, I've been a duke in a tux, a cowboy, and a chef."

"Fun, isn't it?" says Hilde. "What was your favorite?"

"One year, Bill and I dressed as pumpkins for a neighborhood party. We wore orange sheets with elastic at top and bottom. Our boys stood on the bed and stuffed them with newspapers. We could hardly walk without bumping into something or someone."

Hilde laughs. "I felt that way when I was Dolly Parton."

Chapter Seven

1957-1958
Arzberg, Germany

While Sputnik was launched and the Space Age began, Bruni was saddled with adult responsibilities.

I wanted to become a beautician which would not have paid a lot of money, so at fifteen I started work at the china factory. I could go to a three year trade school for beauticians, but money was needed at home. I would have to work for three years and get on-the-job training. The owner paid ten dollars per month. Each year he would pay more until graduation.

In the meantime, my mom got sick every year with pneumonia, and diagnosed as eighty-five percent disabled, was not able to work. She had a very large bump on the head from being hit in the concentration camp. Every year the pastor came to our house to bless her because we all thought she would not live long. She had every illness a person could have. We children, my brother and I, had to support my mom. Wadek gave Mom some money. I suppose he could have done better. He wanted to marry Mom, but she said "One time was enough".

Wadek worked like a horse. He expected the same from my brother. At twenty, my brother Helmut worked in construction. He had to hand over his entire paycheck. His friends only paid room and board. They always had spending money. Helmut got an allowance, but he had to buy gasoline for his motorcycle to get to work.

One week he kept money for himself. When mother asked to see his payroll slip, Helmut stalled. Wadek did not. He hauled out and hit Helmut in the back of the neck with his flat hand. Helmut passed out and fell to the floor. My sister Anneliese and her husband Hans, and Grandmother had been visiting and watched the whole commotion. Grandmother went berserk and confronted Wadek. My sister was about eight months pregnant then with her third baby. She broke down and cried, so did I. My mother was silent and watched.

Wadek advanced on Anneliese. Hans stepped between them "I'll kill you if you harm my pregnant wife."

Grandmother Maria started screaming at Wadek, "You leave her alone you, *Swinehund.*" Wadek really lost his temper raising his arm to strike Grandma. Mom told Grandma to get out. It was a nightmare. We finally revived Helmut, he cried. We all cried except my mother and Wadek. My grandmother left the house.

It would be two years until grandmother would see my mother again. My brother and I would periodically walk up the hill to where my grandmother and grandfather Simon lived. Most of the time we went there because we were hungry and grandmother would feed us her wonderful home-cooked meals. At the same time I could visit my sister and brother-in-law and their three children.

Mom said that I needed to work at the town's Schumann china factory because I would make the most money there. Doing piecework, I did not get paid per hour. To make money, I had to put out a lot of china, painting a rim around the cup or saucer with gold or silver and putting pictures onto the plates and other items.

After Konfirmation, I went to school one day a week and studied Home Economics and graduated at seventeen. I worked four-and-a half days per week at the factory.

My grandfather Simon also worked at the china factory. Lots of times I would go to his department to see him or to have lunch with him. Most of the time, I didn't have a lunch because my mother didn't have money to buy groceries. Wadek wanted us to eat rye bread and drink black coffee. Grandpa would look at me and ask "Once again you don't have anything to eat. Didn't your mother make you a lunch?" I was starving. Grandma would always bring Grandpa a hot dinner for lunchtime, so he would give me his lunch money and tell me to go to the cafeteria to buy something.

Grandpa Simon was special to me always and I was special to him. Many times he comforted me when I cried about the way my mother treated me and how I hated my home life. I did not like Wadek. He took over and acted like he was my father when my mother was not even married to him.

I worked at the factory nine hours daily with one hour for lunch in between, so everyday I was at the factory ten hours. On Saturday I started work at seven in the morning. When I got home, I was ordered to do all the housework. On Sunday it was the same, doing dishes, washing floors, doing laundry. I did all that at fifteen.

***

By the time I was sixteen, life became unbearable at home. My mother lived in her bedroom complaining of headaches. Daily we went to work and she stayed in bed. We didn't know what to think or do. When I came home from work, I started to do some housework. Sometimes, I cleaned the entire house.

When Mom was in a good mood, she would give me permission to go out. Sunday afternoons, I went to a disco. We drank apple cider or grape juice and danced to Rock and Roll, Tango or Foxtrot. I was a very good dancer and had no trouble getting a dance partner.

Other times when I wanted to go to a dance, Mom told me I could go after I did the dishes. Next she said I could get ready for the dance after I scrubbed the stairs outside. It was a very cold winter when I scrubbed those steps. I hated everything about my life because by the time I was done with the chores, it was too late for me to get ready for the dance or to catch the train.

My mother ordered chores out of spite. At that time she said, "You don't deserve to do all those things because I never had the opportunity to do those things when I was growing up". I also didn't deserve a dress or shoes or coat because she never got them. It was unfair for her to think that way about me and my brother.

One Sunday a very good looking boy I'd never seen before asked me to dance. I was very surprised when he introduced himself as Manfred and told me he came from Marktredwitz, my hometown. He came to Arzberg by train with a friend Hans. We danced and talked. My girlfriend Gisela was with me and Manfred introduced Gisela to Hans. The time went by so fast. At ten o'clock Manfred and Hans had to walk to the train station. I was so glad when Manfred asked for a date for next Sunday. He was eighteen with black hair and brown eyes. He was about 5"4". I thought I never saw a better looking guy, he was so kind and sweet.

A few days after we met I was surprised to receive a letter from him. Mom was happy for me. Sometimes she would be nice and approved of me. So the next Sunday Manfred and I saw each other again. Hans came and met up with Gisela. We took a long walk to Elisenfels, through the valley where my father was shooting at us. We held hands and laughed. We stopped and admired the flowers and little creatures on the ground. We picked hazelnuts from the tree and ate them. When we reached the restaurant in Elisenfels, Manfred told me to order something to eat. We ate and listened to *Musik* and danced. The day went by so fast. We set out to walk back to Arzberg and Manfred dropped me off at my door before he and Hans went to the train station.

I cannot explain how happy I was. For the first time someone really liked me for me, and I noticed how the girls in town were surprised that I had a good looking and nice boyfriend.

One day my mother felt better and Grandma and Grandpa wanted to go for a walk into the valley to go to the same restaurant. Mom and Waldek, Helmut and Manfred and I went along. Nobody argued when Grandpa Simon was around. He would not tolerate fighting. He was such an imposing man. Oh, how I loved him. He was like a father. The one I never had. My family liked Manfred, too.

One girl I really liked was Brigitte. She was beautiful. She had red hair and sensational legs. She lived in a small town near the border and walked to my school about five kilometers. People said she looked like Brigette Bardot and I think they were right. One day Brigitte said "Bruni, Let's go see a fortune teller. She can read in the cards what your future will bring." So I said, "Oh, I want her to tell me that this miserable existence is coming to an end soon."

When we sat at the fortune teller's table, first it was Brigitte's turn. She told her that she was going to marry a German man and have lots of kids. Brigitte did not want to hear that, for she was dating an *Amerikan* soldier and wanted to marry him and go to *Amerika*. Since she lived right on the border of *Tschelslovakia* she met some of the soldiers.

I didn't want to marry any *Amerikan*. I was only sixteen and dating Manfred whom I liked very much. When it was my turn, the fortune teller told me that I will meet a tall man, with brown hair and blue eyes and I will take a long journey over a large body of water with him. I did not know at all what that meant. Brigitte was very angry for my fortune is what she wanted to hear. She wanted to go to the U.S. not marry a German and have a bunch of kids. So we left not knowing what to make of it. Little did I know. The fortune teller was right.

One Sunday Manfred and Hans came to Arzberg. Gisela and I met them at the train station. We walked all the way into town to the disco. We were holding hands and looked dreamily at each other. I was so in love.

I noticed that Manfred was looking behind him sometimes and so was Hans. I didn't know what to think of it. When we came into the disco, I noticed two ladies had followed us. Manfred acted nervous. We danced and laughed and talked, but those two ladies kept watching us. Manfred did not say anything, so Gisela and I tried to ignore the women.

Manfred and Hans said good-bye at the disco and went to the train station sooner. The two ladies also left. For several days I kept thinking about this odd occurrence, but I didn't know what to think. The following week when I got home from work on Friday, I found a letter from Manfred in the mailbox. I was as always happy to hear from him, so I couldn't wait to open the letter.

As I read the first lines, I started to get alarmed because this letter didn't sound like all the other loving and sweet letters I received in the past from him. I sat on the stairs and read the letter over and over. I felt like smacking my forehead for I did not understand what it all meant. It had all those odd words and it didn't make sense to me. Finally, it hit me in the middle of my chest.

A heavy and dull feeling overtook me. Dizzy, I couldn't get my breath. I cried. I put my face in my hands to muffle my sobs. I stayed on the stairs for a long time for I didn't want to be with anyone or be seen.

Manfred wrote, "The ladies last Sunday were my mother and Hans' mom. They wanted to come to Arzberg and observe Gisela and you. I was told not to tell you." His mother found out that I was the daughter of Ludwig Maurer who lived in Marktredwitz. Manfred's father, Herr Hecht, had a business selling coal and wood. Manfred worked for him. He delivered coal and wood by trade to various customers in town.

When business was good and they got very busy, they would hire my *Vater*. Frau Hecht knew my father well and his reputation. She knew about the shooting. *Vater* still liked to go to bars and make a fool of himself. And he was divorced. In those days people looked down on the divorced. My *Vater* was always seen with different women. Frau Hecht forbade Manfred to see me again.

On a later Sunday Manfred made an effort to dress up and meet me at the train station. Gisela and I went there. Only Hans appeared in the door of the compartment and I waited to see Manfred. When Hans came to the gate alone, I knew Manfred was not coming. Hans told me that Frau Hecht took Manfred's good suit and shoes and did not give him his allowance.

I received another letter in which Manfred apologized for not coming. He asked me to wait for him for three years until he was twenty-one and we would marry.

Things got worse at home. With Mom's terrible headaches, she couldn't remember things. She was in horrible pain, held her head in both hands and cried out loud. We were helpless.

The doctor said she needed stronger glasses. But with them the pain still didn't go away. So she walked to the doctor's office and collapsed in the middle of Main Street. Someone carried her home. We had to go to work and Mom was alone. We waited for the doctor to admit Mom to the hospital in another town about 150 kilometers away. We never knew why he didn't admit her then. We think he was a Hitler lover.

One day I came home from work, Grandma was there at the house and she was upset. She didn't know that Mom was so ill. They had not been talking for two years since Mom showed her the door when Wadek had knocked my brother Helmut out. Grandma told my brother-in-law John to call the clinic in Erlangen to find out if they could take Mom there. "Yes", they told him, "Bring her right away".

We hired an ambulance and Grandma told me to give Mom a bed bath. I cleaned her body and put on her pinstriped suit with a white blouse. I was so young and naïve. I didn't know what to think. When Mom was dressed and I combed her beautiful black hair, Wadek, Hans, and Helmut carried Mom down the narrow steps into the ambulance. It never occurred to me that when the doors closed on that ambulance that I would never see Mom alive again.

Three days later I was home on vacation from work, sleeping at ten in the morning. There was a knock at the door. I got up, got dressed quickly and saw Mr. Haas our policeman standing at the door. I opened the door and he gave me the sad news that Mom had passed during the night. They had opened her head and saw that a tumor had gotten so large that it had suffocated her brain. She was forty-four years old. I was seventeen.

I must have been in shock, for like a robot, I took the house keys and walked through the backyard to Grandma's to tell her the sad news. Some of the old neighbor ladies sat nearby on a bench and on chairs chatting daily from morning till late at night. I was almost past them when Rosa, a little skinny lady with a goiter and a hump back, stopped me.

She put an arm around me and said. "Go back to the house. Change clothes". I asked her why. "You should not wear a red skirt and red shoes, it isn't proper," she said. The other ladies nodded and said, "Wear dark clothing." I didn't notice what clothes I was wearing. I went into the house and changed to a black skirt and black top. About halfway up the hill, I saw Grandma coming down. The policeman had informed her also. We walked back to the house and made arrangements to bring Mom's body home.

Helmut came later that afternoon. He had changed jobs and had driven a truck with his boss to Nürnberg picking up produce for a fruit and vegetable business. There they gave him the news about an emergency at home and he kept saying "Tell me what's wrong at home. Did my mother die?"

When his boss told him the news, Helmut collapsed. All the way home about 150 kilometers, he cried and cried. He was twenty-years-old and really cared for Mom more than I did, I guess. He could not control himself so his boss drove the truck home.

I was not able to cry and did not cry for six weeks. Everyone else sobbed. Wadek cried for days. One morning I saw him wash his face in the washbowl and tears just dropped into the water.

A lot of people came to the funeral. Mom looked beautiful in a dark suit. She didn't look dead. Her cheeks were rosy and her hair was pulled back off her face. She still wore the ring Robert her Ukraine lover had given her a long time ago. She had told me once that "Robert was the only man I ever loved." The ring was embedded in her finger. She had gained weight and the hand swelled, yet she refused to have Robert's ring removed.

Helmut walked between my sister and me behind the hearse. We followed it from the house all the way up the hill to the church and the cemetery. At the gravesite, Anneliese and I stood on each side of Helmut holding him up. We didn't know what he was going to do.

It was decided that he and I would live with Wadek in our apartment, but as time went on, Helmut wouldn't go to work sometimes a week at a time. He didn't care anymore and was mourning Mom's death. We never knew that he loved her so much for he never showed her any affection. He'd caused her trouble. Mom could never punish him or hit him. She would find a reason to beat me up when Helmut made her angry. She had to relieve her frustrations, so she would get the belt and beat me for a very small incident or times when I would defend Helmut. At times, she kicked me on the floor. She could be a strong woman.

Fifty years ago people didn't know what manic depression or bi-polar was and I guess that's what my mother suffered from with all the illnesses and depression she suffered. I understand today the reason why she always stayed in bed for weeks at a time. And she suffered, too, from what she had to endure in the concentration camp.

People in town also talked about Mom because of her confinement there and her past marriage. It was not long after the war and people still remembered Mom's troubles.

When I was a teenager, I learned from Mom that *Oma* had written a letter to my *Vater* about her and Robert. "But why did *Oma* report you? I don't understand."

"If the SS found out that she knew and didn't tell," she said. "She'd be sent away too." *Oma* was religious and didn't approve of adultery.

Wadek didn't mourn Mom very long. Six months after Mom died he married a young Polish woman he'd had an affair with while Mom was dying. People told me that they would see him on Sunday afternoons riding up a hill leading to a small town where the young Polish woman lived. He had bought a moped, so he wore boots and knickers and a nice jacket when he went to see this woman. That was a moment when I found out again that I could not trust my father or Wadek. They both were womanizers.

Things worsened between Helmut and Wadek because Helmut wouldn't go to work. Wadek didn't want to support Helmut, so Helmut went to live with Grandma and Grandpa. He did go to work daily while he lived with them. Grandma took good care of him. That left Wadek and me in the apartment. He expected me to cook for both of us when I got home from work. I was tired after nine hours in the factory. At seventeen, I worked fifty hours a week in the factory and had to maintain the apartment and cook.

About one month after Mom died, Gisela and I decided to go to a restaurant on a Saturday evening for sauerkraut and bratwurst. As we went in, the *Gasthaus* was full of guys. We didn't know a soccer team from Fichtelberg was in town. They were playing the next day in our town. Gisela and I found a couple of seats at a table in the corner. A bunch of guys and a few girls sat at our table.

Across from me sat a good looking guy and a redhead. They introduced themselves. The guy's name was Heinrich, Heinz for short. He kept looking at me and smiled a lot. I still wore black clothing, so he knew I was in mourning. Somehow I mentioned to him that my mother passed away. He actually ignored his redhead girlfriend and tried to carry on a conversation with me.

I was not interested for I still cried every night for Manfred. I loved him with all of my heart and I missed him. Before Mom passed on, I would cry every night for Manfred and the next day I had to go to work. With swollen and red eyes, I arrived at the factory. When my co-workers noticed they would say, "What's wrong?" Did your mother beat you again?" So I lied and said "Yes" because I didn't want them to know that I was crying over a boy.

I forgot about this guy Heinz, little did I know how I was going to get mixed up with him and how I was going to regret it.

Bruni's school in Arzberg where she attended
from ages 7-14, second grade to Konfirmation

Chapter Eight

1954-1958
Aliquippa, Pennsylvania

While Eisenhower was president and school desegregation began, Peggy started the busiest years of her life with school and outside activities.

Lynn, Elaine and I were separated again in different homerooms, but we continued meeting everyday to sit on the gym bleachers and eat brown bag lunches. Afterwards, we walked off campus to a small store for snacks, or met in an upstairs hall and wide-eyed and gasping, read chapters of the forbidden book, Peyton Place, "Can you believe she wrote this?" or attend study sessions for college placement tests "These questions are hard!" Long phone calls with each other became common after school. "Did you see who was holding hands today?" We held slumber parties for any occasion and discussed boys, hair styles and clothes.

My homeroom, Mrs. Fleming's, was a friendly mixture of academic, commercial and vocational students who helped each other with homework and classes during our four years together. One summer I "crewed" on Mrs. Fleming's yacht. Her husband had broken his leg and wasn't able to crew. I learned boating on the job, got a great tan and enjoyed the peacefulness of the water.

Girl's Chorus was the first organization I joined as an alto in my freshman year. In my senior year I became student conductor which pleased my mother, the musician. Four or five of us girls would get together Sunday afternoons at Sandy's apartment downtown and harmonize for fun. Sandy played piano. My mother would transpose music into three part harmony for us. We surprised ourselves at how good we sounded.

I was active in the Pep club making banners for athletic activities and cheering at pep rallies, representing my homeroom for student council, working on the school yearbook scheduling club photos, acting as a stern social worker in the senior play, and speaking at graduation. Lynn, Elaine, Sandy, Julie and Joanne and I bowled in an after school league. We had fun "dating" in a group of an equal number of boys and girls, going to parties, sled riding and picnicking. When some of these friends paired off, dated or went steady, they saw me as the listener to their problems. I tried not to be jealous or judgmental as I knew and liked them all and had my own "secret" crushes.

Again I knew I was being watched in school as my mother knew all the teachers and my dad was still on the school board. I felt an additional obligation to do well as the daughter of an only son. My parents and I had many arguments about my doing something on my own without their help, their names being mentioned or their making the arrangements. Yet one time I forgot to turn in a book report and got my lowest grade. I walked downtown to the bank to go home that evening with my dad, afraid to face my mom alone! I needed his help!

In these same weeks and months, I worked at a deli/bakery on the Terrace. I would walk down the alley in my white uniform and work behind the counter, slicing lunch meat, selling candy and helping display bake goods. I gained a lot of weight that summer as I always took home an iced chocolate roll. One time, I sat in the back of the station wagon holding a three tiered wedding cake stable between my legs. That summer I cut my finger on the meat cutter, learned quickly how to make change and balance the till and that the customer is always right.

Some nights we'd be awakened in the middle of the night by a phone call for my dad from the local police station. The bank's alarm had sounded. The police came to the house and took my dad downtown to the bank to shut off the alarm. It was always embarrassing to have the police car drive to the house and pick up my dad in the middle of the night! I was shocked to see in newsreels that, at the same time, men in other countries were being picked up by the police at night and never seen again. After that revelation, I could never complain nor tease my dad about his nighttime police rides.

Summers, I volunteered as a "candy striper" in the newly opened Aliquippa Hospital. Using my past experience behind the counter I worked in the gift shop, sold snacks, gifts and delivered flowers to patients. I wore my red and white apron proudly and tried to be helpful. It was rewarding to be helping others who were sick, but I knew I could never be a doctor or nurse.

Some weekends, I babysat for a family with five boys. The father lined them all up and showed me where to hit each one where it hurt. I had no trouble with the boys.

Babysitting was not always that easy. I also baby sat for my Aunt Rene's children and caught the chicken pox. Extremely sick, I had scabs everywhere even on my eyelids. Schoolwork was sent home, I tried to keep up with assignments. My mother read to me everyday from a collection of Mark Twain stories, "The Jumping Frog of Calaveras County", "Puddinghead Jones", "The Prince and the Pauper" and the account of Sir Edmund Hillary's conquest of Mt. Everest. Mother had also joined a book of the month club and we read the latest books Agony and Ecstasy, biography of Michelangelo, and Love is Eternal, story of Lincoln's marriage. I listened to the radio for many hours. An old crystal radio my dad built had wires attached to my bedsprings and reception depended on my position in bed. Daytimes I listened to soaps. Nighttimes, I listened to ball games and a call-in show with Ed and Wendy King with their lilting theme song, a selection from Rachmaninoff's "A Theme from Paganini".

My dad led me to an interest in baseball. I would listen to afternoon Pittsburgh Pirates games and report scores to him when he came home from work. He and I also went into the city and Forbes Field for Pittsburgh Pirate games. I saw Jackie Robinson play on the opposing team and once spotted Pirate players for a sports reporter. My mother didn't like sports and one time, sitting in the stands, read a book during a game. One hot week in summer I spent in the basement listening to Pittsburgh Pirate games as I white-washed the walls, the coolest place to be with an exciting interest to take my mind off a tedious job.

I attended football and basketball games with my friends. Football reigned as king on Friday nights in Aliquippa. Competition in Beaver

Valley was fierce and produced many good players: Joe Namath, Mike Ditka, Tony Dorsett. Football was their way out of spending a life working in the mill. At games, we would shout ourselves hoarse led by our friend Julie, a cheerleader. My dad taught me the elements of the games from a chalkboard propped against the wall in our dining room. He would diagram plays "Put the quarterback in the pocket" and explain the positions, "Name the linemen." Not having a son to play the game, Dad wanted his daughter to be a knowledgeable fan! He also used the chalkboard to teach me math. "Add 12345 and 678910." He'd say grinning. Fascinated with numbers, he couldn't understand why I was not. I struggled to make average grades in algebra and geometry.

At sixteen, I was ready to drive a car, but had to wait for second semester when I could take in-school classes. My instructor was more confident than I. On my first day behind the wheel, he sat in the passenger seat, opened a newspaper and began to read it, and said, "Drive." I had to rely on what I'd seen my parents do! After school, I learned to parallel park the car between metal chairs Mother sat in front of our house. The neighbors knew when I hit a metal chair. From its clanging as it hit the street, I learned quickly how to parallel park! "I can do this" was my mantra. I passed my driver's test on my first try.

Real tests came when I had my license and drove alone. I accused my dad of having every policeman in town watching me. Dad was the borough treasurer and knew the men on the force. I had no accidents, nor tickets, and was always looking in my rearview mirror, conscious of keeping the family name clean.

That year, my mother arranged for my first plane ride in a small private plane. The pilot took me over Aliquippa. I enjoyed the trip until he flew over the smoke stacks of the Jones&Laughlin steel plant. The bumpiness made me queasy and the trip became scary. From then on, I would fly only to get somewhere quickly. Every bump, jolt or shudder of a plane made me motion-sick. I shouldn't have been surprised. There were times when I got car-sick and my parents would have to stop driving for me to vomit on the side of the road. Other times Mother would drive to Aunt Edna's and Uncle Paul's and take the dog and me. We both got car-sick!

Christmas vacation of my senior year, Mother, Aunt Ola and I flew to New York City to see the city decorated for the holiday. The store windows and the city were larger and more beautiful than I'd ever seen! My cousin, Bill Craig, lived there and made hotel arrangements and for us to see Rockefeller Center and the huge tree, the Rockettes at Radio City Music Hall, and to eat at a French restaurant in Central Park. (I was taking French classes.) We attended Mass at St. Patrick's and heard Bill sing in the choir at an Episcopal church. Back home, I stood a little straighter and felt very sophisticated and worldly for having traveled if only one state away!

Summers weren't all spent working and babysitting. My family continued to go to Lake Erie with Aunt Edna and Uncle Paul and the twins, cherry picking then swimming in Lake Erie with my Aunt Ola, Aunt Clara and Uncle Joe and my Leis cousins. Saturday nights we'd go square dancing. I would still spend a week at Aunt Clara and Uncle Joe's farm. My parents took me there and my uncle would bring me back to town on his way to work. He would always stop at a small store to "see a man about a dog". I never guessed he was going in for a drink. I never saw a dog.

On one trip, Dad came to pick me up and in the car said, "Your mother had to put Spot to sleep." I dissolved into tears sobbing, "How could she do that? He was my dog, too!" I cried the whole way home. Dad didn't say a word and let me cry. I didn't speak to Mother for days. I was angry at her that she sent Dad to tell me, angry that I didn't know my dog was sick.

Mother, Dad and I took vacations touring historical places, New York and the Statue of Liberty, the Skyline Drive and the caverns in Virginia, Philadelphia and Independence Hall, Washington DC. and Mt. Vernon. In these places I learned the value of taking guided tours to see all in a short amount of time. People in history have always fascinated me as I tried to imagine living in their places in their time.

One Halloween my parents set up a spook house in the garage for a Halloween party. They had a good time blindfolding me and my friends, handing us spaghetti "intestines", grape "eyeballs" and real liver "organs" as we were led through wet strips of crepe paper hung from the rafters. Mine and my friends' parents were involved in our lives hosting fun parties, yet establishing rules and expectations with consequences if not met. I was "grounded" once for a week for not calling in to say I would be late driving home from somewhere. As I walked in the door, I handed over the car keys into my dad's open hand. I didn't try to argue. I knew I wouldn't see the keys for a week.

Proms were important events. For my junior prom I went with my cousin who had just moved into Aliquippa. Knowing I didn't have a date and his being new in town, he and I decided to go together. As a new student, he was not known as my cousin. I wore a borrowed pink gown, had shoulder length hair and didn't smile in photos. We went out afterwards to eat with two other couples. I didn't go to my senior prom. I didn't have a date. I had worked weeks planning and decorating the gym and was feeling sorry for myself. My dad took me to the movies in another town that night. I didn't want to be seen in Aliquippa. I was embarrassed to be dateless and couldn't wait for the next day's reports of the evening from Lynn and Elaine.

In all of this activity, I made good grades and was elected to the National Honor Society in my junior year. This was the first time I was called Margaret in school and sat in my seat when my name was called. My name had to be called twice. Nudged by my homeroom friends, tapped on the shoulder by Mrs. Fleming, I realized Margaret was me! I didn't know I had been nominated. I had not seen the envelope with the letter to my parents inviting them to the ceremony. Many letters from the school system came to our house because of my dad's position as a school board member. Although it was my job to bring in the mail, I felt stupid for not suspecting one envelope addressed to BOTH my parents. The name Margaret followed me to college. I quickly changed it to Peggy.

Senior year was also filled with college prep courses, practicing for senior play and graduation speeches, taking college entrance exams, completing applications and making college visits. A teacher from high school took three of us seniors for a weekend look at a small college, and Mother and I visited two other colleges and a state university. I was accepted and earned a scholarship at Grove City College, a small college and my mother's alma mater.

My father wasn't sure that college was for girls. He saw young girls train for months for positions at the bank, then marry and quit. Mother and I assured him that a college education would help me all through life. We made a pact, he would agree to pay for my education if I graduated and worked two years out of college before I married.

Lynn and Elaine and I were separated again as we headed for different colleges.

While NASA was established and Explorer I launched, it was time for me to enter a new world, leave family and friends and enter into college life.

During a Christmastime lunch Hilde hands me a flat box.

I open it to find a china cake plate with matching server trimmed with miniature snowmen.

"I know you bake a fruitcake for the holiday and could use this," she says.

We talked many lunch times about how I make the cake the day after Thanksgiving and how hard it is to find its secret ingredient.

She licks her lips. "What did you soak it in this year?"

"What ever we have the most of in the liquor cabinet," I say.

I hand her a Christmas bonus and wish her a Merry Christmas.

"I'll renew my membership to the gym with this," she says.

"And I'll think of you when I serve from this plate," I say.

"And what else?"

"I have a list of cookies I bake every year."

"Like what?"

"When all are here at Thanksgiving, we make Buckeyes-peanut butter balls dipped in chocolate."

"Why then?"

"My recipe is for seventy-five. Everyone helps. One day we roll the peanut butter balls, freeze them, and the next day we dip them in chocolate and freeze again."

"Are they ready to serve?" Hilde asks. "I'd like one."

Chapter Nine

1959-1960
Marktredwitz and Fichtelberg, Germany

While Castro came into power in Cuba and Konrad Adenauer was Chancellor of Germany, Bruni's life fell apart.

A week after I met Heinz, I received a letter from Manfred. "I heard about your mother's death. I want to come and talk to you."

On a Sunday about one o'clock I walked to the train station to meet Manfred. I was so happy to see him. He hugged me and told me how sorry he was. We took a walk and went to eat at a restaurant. I was already very upset because I noticed a gold ring on his left ring finger. In Germany you wore a ring on your left hand if you are engaged and the gold band on the right hand if you are married. In the restaurant he explained to me that his mother forced him to get engaged to a girl whose parents also have a coal and wood business. The business that Manfred's parents owned was not going well, for Mr. Hecht spent most of his time in a *Gasthaus* playing poker for money.

After meeting with Manfred, I was devastated about his engagement. I knew that he did not love this girl. After I married, Manfred broke up with her, but it was too late for us.

I had to move out of the apartment. Wadek married his Polish girl. She moved into my mother's place.

Heinz kept asking me to marry him. "We could live in my mother's boyfriend Joseph's house. You would have a place and a husband to care for you", he said.

I did not know where to turn. I could not go to my grandmother's house. There was no room. It was hard to find a room. No one would rent a place to a single young girl. So we planned a wedding. Heinz gave me an engagement ring in November. In April 1959 we got married. I was eighteen.

We had a white wedding. I was not in love although I thought I was. When I walked down the aisle, I cried. I had a very strong feeling that I was doing the wrong thing. I would be in for a nightmare which would change my personality and my spirit. I was not able to laugh and be carefree any longer. Heinz was intoxicated by eleven o'clock on our wedding day. We hired a limousine and drove to Marktredwitz where I was born. We could not get married in the Catholic Church in Fichtelberg where Heinz lived. It was Lent.

There was a bus for all of the wedding guests to ride to Marktredwitz. My *Vater* and his second wife, Agnes, my sister and brother-in-law and a couple of my girlfriends were invited. My grandfather Simon and Grandma were not able to attend. Simon had severe colitis. They decided not to come to the wedding or reception at a restaurant. We invited about ninety-five guests, all relatives of Heinz family. It already began to dawn on me that my mother-in-law was going to make all the decisions for me and Heinz. He was already drunk and argumentative. We had *Zither Musik* (table guitars). It was very nice and people danced.

I looked pretty in my white dress. I had hired a seamstress to make it. Heinz bought me a beautiful bouquet of roses. Dressed in a black suit, he was very handsome. He was tall and slender with black curly hair and dark eyes. If only he would not have been drunk, we could have had a wonderful wedding and I could have loved him.

During the dinner and the festivities, people came from all over the community to the *Gasthaus* and congratulated us. Later when the music started, all the males lined up to ask the bride for a dance. That was the custom in my country. The males asked Heinz if they were allowed to dance with the bride. "Of course," Heinz said." You may dance with my wife." I sat beside him at the center of the table and at the same time he pinched me on my thigh very hard. He said I was to say "No" to the guy. The fellow looked at me very startled wondering why I said no when it was the custom to dance with the bride. He didn't see Heinz pinch me under the table. I was afraid to stand up and dance. Already I was terrified of Heinz. His dark eyes could look very piercing. So it went with all the fellows, each one walked away in bewilderment. Then it was said in town that Heinz new wife was very stand-uppish, prudish. It was humiliating.

Late in the evening someone drove us home. Heinz was loaded and I was tired. I was standing in the bedroom. I couldn't get out of my wedding dress for it had buttons down my back from the top to the lower waist. Heinz fell into bed and fell asleep immediately. After awhile I had no choice but to lie down in my dress.

Already I was sorry with a foreboding of worse times.

My sister and brother-in-law, as well as my father and his new wife Agnes, were not invited to stay over night at Joseph's house. Although there was enough room at the house where Heinz and I lived, my family had to stay at the train station until five o'clock in the morning to wait for the train's arrival. I felt sorry for them but there was nothing I could say. It was up to Maria, my mother-in-law to invite them. The next morning, Heinz finally was sober, he got up and dressed to meet a friend. They brought all the wedding gifts from Maria's house to our home. Heinz didn't have a car, so they made about ten trips, one half mile each to bring the presents home.

When we had sex, it was not very good. I hated it for I did not know much about love-making. No one ever explained anything to me and Heinz was very impatient with me. Although he had been around, I found out, he was very inconsiderate and selfish. I endured his advances and I always was afraid for he cussed me out while he was doing it to me. Pretty soon in our marriage he would not get up to go to work. He would get home late, around three in the morning from the beer joint or *Gasthaus* where he drank and played cards or danced with other women.

I got a job in Fichtelberg and went to work daily. Often I was late getting to work because Heinz would wake me up at two or three when he fell up the stairs and I was tired from taking care of him. Often he would sing very loudly and cuss waking up all the neighbors. As soon as he got in the door, Heinz started arguing and looking in all the corners for a man. He accused me of having men in the bedroom while he was in the bar. He said I was having sex for money with those guys. On and on he went. Then he forced me to have sex and called me names. I was eighteen. I was stunned. I didn't know what the hell had happened to me and what I got myself into. It was all a bad dream and I hoped to wake up anytime.

We were married about a month when I was sick every morning. I didn't know I was pregnant. I was so naïve and dumb. I tried to cook dinners every evening when I got home from work. Most of the time, Heinz didn't come home. He went straight to a bar after work. I soon found out that he didn't go to work at all in the morning. He pretended he was going to town to meet the train and waited in front of the bar for it to open. I went to work with the belief that Heinz was at work too. Most of the time, he would only work three days per week. When he received his paycheck, he went straight to the bar on Friday and came home broke. This went on for months.

A few months had passed when he started choking me because he didn't like the meal I cooked. I didn't like to cook when I got home and I was not very experienced. Several times, grabbing a fork and holding it to my neck, he would yell, "Why can't you cook as well as my mother? She cooked for a restaurant".

One time when we went to a neighborhood restaurant to eat, we sat by a window where people would pass. If I looked up from my plate and looked out the window when a man passed by, Heinz would kick me very hard in the shins whispering "Stop eyeing the other man. You are nothing but a whore for lusting after other men". It was sickening. I was pregnant and my legs hurt badly. I wanted to throw up right into the plate.

I could not go anywhere with him. He was always drinking. One Saturday night we went with Mother-in-law and her boyfriend Joseph to a dance at a *Gasthaus*. We had a good dinner and afterward Maria went up to the band and sang the song "Tom Dooley". She had a beautiful voice and was known for her singing. About two in the morning we went home. Maria and Joseph went the other direction towards their home.

As soon as they were around the corner, Heinz took off ahead of me. It was dark and we went through a wooded area, I was afraid and five months pregnant. I wore shoes with heels, and could not see well in the dark. Heinz was running ahead of me and hollering, "C'mon, keep up." I tried to keep up with him. As I ran after him, I fell into a hole with one foot and could not get out. "Heinz, stop, I've fallen," I yelled to him but he ignored me. So I made my way home alone in the dark. When I finally reached the house, Heinz started screaming and demanding, "What took you so long?" It was unreal. I tried to explain what happened. It didn't make any difference to him. He was absolutely crazy. We argued and I cried.

Suddenly he grabbed a rope. "I'm going to hang myself." He ran out of the house towards the barn. I was terrified and believed him. I ran down the stairs after him, through the yard and into the barn. It was pitch dark and I could not see where he went. Finally I got adjusted to the darkness in the barn and I saw him hanging there. I screamed, "Heinz, Heinz, why are you doing this?" I rushed up to him to undo the rope.

In the dark I could not see that he had one arm around the pole and was holding on. Finally after I screamed for an eternity for him, he jumped down from the loft. "Ha, scared you didn't I?" he said and laughed and laughed like a mad man. I felt like my baby was going to burst out of my belly, I was terrified and puzzled. I could not understand how a *Mensch* could act this way. I was convinced that he was the devil in disguise. He was evil. I hated him with a passion.

Heinz left me standing there and took off into the house. I just stood there forever holding my belly, trying to make sense of all this craziness and hell I walked into. I knew then that I never loved this horrible man and that I never would. I had no idea that Heinz had such a drinking problem. He had just been released from a hospital where he got treatment for his drinking. No one told me. His mother was glad to be rid of him.

When I was seven and a half months into my pregnancy, I took maternity leave from my job in the china factory. The law read that pregnant women had to take leave six weeks before and eight weeks after the child was born with pay. In those days a woman did not go to the doctor during pregnancy. I saw the mid-wife at the beginning of the pregnancy. She guessed at the birth date. On the morning of August 13, I walked to my mother-in-law's house down the hill with Heinz. I had the feeling it was time for the baby to come. I was in a fog. I could hardly walk. At Maria's house, she whispered to Heinz that I may be going into labor soon. I kept going to the bathroom. At five in the evening I told Heinz that I wanted to go home. We made it up the hill and I was able to lie down. Several hours later I got up and walked across the room when my water broke. I did not know what that meant. Heinz ran back down the hill and brought back his mother and notified the mid-wife. I was told to walk around the room. It seemed like an eternity. I had no idea how long it would take for the baby to come. I assumed it would be any moment. Maria prepared the sofa with sheets and a rubber cover. It was midnight and I was sleeping between contractions. The mid-wife arrived. They gave me black coffee to keep me awake. When I was told to push, I did the opposite because it hurt so much. I dozed off until the next contraction. When nothing happened at two o'clock, the mid-wife and the doctor, who had just arrived, decided to oil some equipment to use to take the baby out. Ready for the procedure another contraction began. I was tired and angry because the baby wouldn't come. I pushed and pushed. Suddenly the head appeared and with another push, a ten pound beautiful girl with lots of black hair finally arrived. My husband and mother-in-law held my hand all through this agony. The neighbors said they didn't get any sleep that night because of my screaming. What did they expect? I didn't get any medication. For awhile they thought the baby would be a breech birth. I stayed in bed for two weeks. Heinz had vacation off from work, but he wasn't much help around the house. The second day he went to the bar to brag and stayed out every night until two in the morning. I stayed home alone trying unsuccessfully to breast-feed. Maria and Heinz decided to name the baby Petra Amelia. I had no say.

Maria's sister in Nürnberg wanted to be the godmother. This was a good thing. They had a large clothing store and supplied us with all the baby's clothes and other things. We also got many things for the household from Aunt Amelia for our wedding. Heinz had a wonderful job in tool and dye making. He went to school in Nürnberg at fifteen to learn the profession. He lived with his aunt there. We could have had a good marriage and a good living. Because of his drinking and absence from work, he hardly brought home a paycheck. When the baby was three weeks old, Maria made arrangements to have Petra baptized in the Catholic church. We had a wonderful party and lots of food. My mother-in-law and the godmother paid for everything.

There was only my pay from the maternity leave. It was the regular pay I would have received if I was working. I paid rent and utilities. When Petra was eight weeks old, I started working at a plant in Fichtelberg. I soldered wires into an object which was installed into a beautiful stereo that looked like a piece of furniture with four legs. It had a record player and a radio. I did piece work and took home a pretty good paycheck.

Heinz accused me of having sex with other men for money. Although I produced the payroll slip, he still maintained that there was no way I could make so much money. No matter how much I tried to convince him that I was faithful, he ranted and raved about what a "slut and whore" I was. Daily I cried and didn't want to live with him any longer. The co-workers kept asking me why a nice and funny girl like me married the village drunk. I didn't know what they meant. It did not occur to me that he was a drunk. At this point I started to understand the whole situation and I realized that my life would never be different with Heinz. I would probably have a house full of children and live in poverty with him.

After six months of living hell, I decided to leave him.

I was nineteen.

Peggy, home from college on surprise visit, presenting family gift
to parents at their 25th wedding anniversary November 1960

Chapter Ten

1958-1962
Chautauqua, New York and Grove City, Pennsylvania

While Nixon visited U.S.S.R and Khrushchev visited the US, and Kennedy was inaugurated president of the United States, Peggy began years away from home.

After high school graduation, at seventeen, I traveled to Lake Chautauqua to look for a summer job to help pay my college expenses. Mother drove a school friend and me the six hours north to New York.

Chautauqua is an educational/spiritual institution in a gated community, a beautiful place of old homes, grand old hotels and restaurants, lecture halls and amphitheaters. The grounds are full of pedestrians, enjoying all the Institute offers for families, conference attendees, students and summer residents. Most businesses employ college students in the summers. My mother and cousin Patty had worked there as college students and wanted me to have a working experience in the same atmosphere.

My friend immediately started work in a hotel laundry and lived in its hotel dormitory. I stayed with Mrs. MacDonald, an eighty-year-old lady who rented a small room off her kitchen. I found a job as a babysitter/housekeeper for three little girls, eight, six and two, whose parents owned and worked in their restaurant. Those first weeks I was extremely homesick, living alone in my small room, working a demanding job and, for the first time, without friends.

One experience did cheer me. I drove the family's Cadillac- the biggest car I ever drove. I couldn't believe my bosses trusted me behind the wheel! They'd never seen me drive. The girls and I got along well and I had the use of the car as long as I included them in the trip.

Overwhelmed with the stress of keeping house and watching three little ones, I would write home and my mother would remind me "Look for the silver lining" a line from a song my friends and I used to sing. I wrote to my college roommate Betty Ann, described the area, and she joined me to work as a waitress at the restaurant.

"Beware of us when we are angry," were the owners' first instructions. He was a temperamental Italian and she, a fiery Irish woman. "Stay out of our way," they said. "We throw things." They fought frequently and loudly. We learned quickly to follow their rules and not be the victim of one of their tirades.

Betty Ann and I rented a room on the top floor of the YWCA on the grounds of Chautauqua Institute. Excited to be part of the summer activities, we would buy a libretto (story) for the week's opera and study it for a Saturday matinee. Sitting in the last row of the balcony, we felt sophisticated and a part of the world of culture. We attended classical and modern concerts on the grounds, took time to soak up sun on the beach, read and enjoy the peaceful surroundings, feeling free and brave.

Between our sophomore and junior years of college, Betty Ann and I both worked as waitresses in the restaurant. We were joined by Elaine (my school friend) and Vera from Aliquippa and lived in a motel room behind the restaurant. Vera had a car. We left town on our days off, shopping for school clothes, sunning and swimming at beaches and sightseeing at Niagara Falls. The car always had a flat tire and, like a NASCAR team, the four of us each had a job and could change a tire quickly and drive on.

Those summers were great experiences in learning how four girls could live in cramped quarters with one bathroom, how to treat all types of customers with a smile, how tired a waitress can be, and how feet could burn and legs could "scream" (my mother's term).

During the last week of our third summer, Betty Ann and I were living in a small house on our boss's property near the restaurant. A wanderer and a drunkard had lived there years before. A big man, he would appear at the restaurant off and on during our summers. Alone in the house one day, I looked up to see him standing at the door rattling the knob.

I feared the worst, he was drunk and would attack me. I ran out the back door towards the restaurant. I had never been so terrified! My boss caught me and made me sit down and tell him what happened. I could only gasp, "He's there. I won't go back." After Joe confronted the man and told him to leave the area, I agreed to go back into the house when Joe made arrangements for the state policeman who patrolled the area to check our little house every day. There were no other incidents, but at times, I can still close my eyes and see the man at the door.

Then back to college.

College years were full of hard work-intense studying, new friends and exciting times. I entered Grove City College without a declared major, not wanting to be a teacher like my mother and all her friends. The first two years consisted of taking core classes for a liberal arts degree. I followed an established program with additional classes in French. Freshman year I lived in an older dorm on the lower campus and walked uphill to classrooms and activities. I lived on the top floor with five girls in a suite of rooms. When we arrived on campus, all of our fathers looked for the fire escape. "It's on the other side," we told them. There was none. We were to crawl out on the roof if there were a fire.

Three freshmen lived on one side of a big bathroom and three sophomores on the other side. Luella (Wella) was one of the sophomores who shared the suite. We had a lot in common and became good friends and traveled to each others homes on long weekends.

An incident in the dorm almost cost me my college career. Girls in one wing of the dorm were upset by a new house rule. In protest, they all agreed to slam their doors at nine one night. One of the jobs as a dorm resident was to "man the phones". I was on phone duty that night. At exactly nine o'clock, a call came in. I paged the person. My voice was not heard over the slamming of doors that shook the whole dorm! I was summoned to the dean's office to face her and the dorm housemother. Trembling I stood before them. "I just answered the phone," I said. "I didn't know the door slamming form of protest". By now, both women knew my name. Again I felt as if I were being watched every day, every year.

College classes opened my eyes to a new world of studying. Good grades came easily in high school. I had to work harder for good grades at this level.

I almost flunked American History 101. The tall professor wearing an eye patch swept into the room at eight o'clock in the morning, leaned against the front of the desk and talked history. Fascinated, I forgot to take notes! Research assignments and written reports kept me afloat in that class.

French 101 began with the professor asking our names and from our accents pinpointing our home area. He was "dead-on". I had taken one year of French in high school and knew I would love this class.

I was dating a track runner that year, a junior, and could watch practices from my dorm room window. He had to explain the new sport to me. He loved track so much that we always ended dates walking around the track before saying goodnight. It was a happy time until he started dating another girl.

Seeing the two of them together on campus was hard to take. Roommates helped me through the break-up. Some had been heartbroken too and survived their loss. Again, I remembered my mother's philosophy, "You can let things happen to you or you can make them happen." I couldn't let his actions get me down and jeopardize my grades. Although I felt discarded, I wouldn't be called "Poor Peggy".

As an only child, I was upset with roommates borrowing my clothes, another new experience. Academically I did well that first year, but studied long hours. I realized how smart others were. I was not in the top part of my class anymore.

My friends joined sororities. I did not. Again, I was the listener. I had friends in different sororities and had fun hearing about and watching the interaction. I was disappointed at not being selected. Part of me wanted to be a "sister", yet I was used to being independent. In retrospect, I wonder if one of the reasons I was not accepted into a sorority was my mail. I probably was the only one receiving Good Housekeeping magazine. Perhaps my mother sent me a subscription to give me something familiar away from home. Now I imagine the college kids sorting mail giggling about my subscription, a housewife's magazine, not a coed's Seventeen, Glamour or Mademoiselle.

After my sophomore year, I declared a major—Elementary Education with a minor in French. I discovered after years of babysitting, I missed working with children and languages came easily. Betty Ann and I were living on upper campus in a beautiful, big, corner room. To one side, it overlooked the arched entranceway to the dorm and the stone patio lined with gorgeous Japanese cherry trees. To the other side, it faced the main quad and its constant activity. Looking up from studying and seeing either of these views was inspiring. We kept the room for two years and so did the girls on the floor below. Betty Ann didn't talk in the mornings and went to early breakfast. She would lift the end of my bed and drop it on her way out of the room. She woke me as well as the girls below. We were their alarm clock!

Junior year began with Education and French classes. In my major now, I made the Dean's List. From studying hard for one day of tests, I mixed the two. Phonetically spelled words were to be translated into English for an education class. I translated them into French. Luckily, the education professor knew French, recognized what I had done and let me retake the test.

Summer of my junior year, I was working at Chautauqua Lake and my parents were vacationing at a cottage at Edinboro Lake in Pennsylvania. My mother drove two hours to New York and back on one of my weekends off and brought me to and from their cottage.

Other Aliquippa families were at Edinboro. The area was known for its good golf courses. My dad was a golfer and loved to play the courses in the area. Saturday morning of the weekend, another Aliquippa person and her son, Bill, who was visiting from college in Pittsburgh, happened to stop at our cottage! I had just awakened. Bleary-eyed, I only saw a tall guy with glasses. Stumbling to the door and wrapped in a blanket with my hair sticking up, I looked like a teepee. I mumbled "Hello".

That evening Bill dropped by. "My family vacations here often. Would you like to see the area?" I was alert then and saw a lanky guy with a blond crew cut and intense eyes behind glasses. We spent the evening together, discovered we had a lot to talk about, we are both only children, went to same high school and church and went to colleges in Pennsylvania. Yet we hadn't known each other. We said a friendly "goodbye". That fall Bill came to Grove City when our college football teams met for a game. He tried to find me, but I was babysitting for a professor's children, my standing Saturday afternoon job. Bill left disappointed. I was oblivious to his visit.

Back home on holiday vacation, Bill and I talked again on New Year's Eve and decided to celebrate together. We realized we had other things in common, his aunt was my dad's secretary, his mom was in my aunt's bridge club and our mothers belonged to the Aliquippa Women's Club. We still couldn't believe we hadn't known each other!

***

Student teaching my senior year was demanding creating lesson plans, student teaching with supervisor observations and critiques, searching for a job and experiencing first formal interviews. In the classroom, I was at ease with the children. One of my mentors asked, "Is your mother a teacher?" When I replied "Yes", she said, "I can tell. You are a natural in the classroom."

I student taught in third and fifth grades in Grove City schools. My supervisor called me in to her office after one evaluation and said. "You need to lower the pitch of your voice to be more effective." I was angry. I stomped out of her office saying, "That's the only voice God gave me." Not until I returned to my dorm did I wonder if I had just ruined my career.

After taking four years of French, I wanted to teach FLES, Foreign Language in Elementary Schools. The program was just starting in some schools and non-existent in others. Spring break of senior year, I interviewed for jobs in my home town and surrounding areas. After the first rejection, I sought refuge at the creek I'd crossed as an elementary student. Along its banks again I watched its continuous flow, still full of minnows and a beaver dam. The same life within reassured me that life goes on.

Bill and I started dating as much as we could when home from colleges. At times, we would take the two-hour bus trip to and from each other's schools for formal dances and stay with friends in other dorms. I invited Bill to a formal dance and sprained my ankle that day. I was devastated. This was to be a great weekend together.

I met him at the Greyhound bus stop seated in the back seat of my friend's car, crutches across my lap. I wore a gown to the dance, sat at a table all evening and spent the weekend on crutches! Later Bill told me he thought I had faked the injury for sympathy. I couldn't believe it! I had excruciating pain in my ankle, red sores in my armpits from not knowing how to walk with crutches and a bruised ego. The doctor said I'd been better off breaking the ankle.

I visited Bill at Carnegie Mellon University, Carnegie Tech at the time, a Pittsburgh city school with a large campus and population. Visits there overwhelmed me. Grove City is a small college on a contained campus. At the time it was about one third the size of Carnegie Tech.

Over the next two years, Bill and I knew we were in love. One day when leaving chapel at Grove City, I smelled the after shave Bill wore and rushed to find who wore it. My head knew it couldn't be Bill, my heart wished it were.

Bill and I planned to marry after we finished school.

Little did we know that would take another two years.

Hilde sits down at the kitchen table.

"Mrs. Hanna, we're washing windows this afternoon."

It is not unusual to be doing one other job in addition to regular house cleaning.

"Why don't you call me Peg?" I ask.

"I call all my clients by their formal names," she says putting down her sandwich.

With raised eyebrows I say, "Even those you've cleaned for, for years?"

She nods. "Of course, cleaning house is a business."

"But you were recommended as Hilde, not Mrs. Barron."

"You are my employer. I work for you."

"In a way, I can understand," I say.

"Oh?"

"When my kids were growing up, it was common to call their friends' mothers by first names. I insisted on being called Mrs. Hanna and insisted my kids call the other mothers Mrs."

Hilde nods.

"I became Mom Hanna to our exchange students and Mrs. H to our kids' young adult friends."

After lunch Hilde rises from the table.

"Now about those windows, Mrs. Hanna, you wash inside. I'll wash outside."

Chapter Eleven

1960-1963
Germany and America

While the Berlin Wall was erected and the Berlin crisis brought the world close to war, Bruni came to the United States.

My mother-in-law took care of my baby girl while I worked. One day I took off early, went to my mother-in-law's house picked up Petra and took her home to our apartment. My husband Heinrich went to the bar as always on Fridays when he got his paycheck. He usually came home at around three in the morning, stone drunk, raising hell, singing and hollering and cussing. The neighbors all along the street heard him at least four times per week.

I packed a suitcase in a hurry and went to the train station with Petra in the baby buggy. I knew Heinrich wouldn't know I left until Saturday morning and not even notice that I was gone until he came out of his stupor the next day.

I rode the train about forty-five kilometers to my grandmother's house. Grandmother was not pleased with my coming. "You can only stay a few days. There is no room for you and the baby." She only had a two room apartment for Grandpa Simon and her. My brother Helmut slept on the sofa in the kitchen/living room combined, but he was out of town working for a few days. Grandma said, "I told you so, Heinz is no good, but you married him anyway." Wise Grandmother caught on to him way before I did. "I didn't like his eyes," she said.

A few days later she sent me to the store into town to get vegetables and fresh meat. I came home about ninety minutes later. The baby was gone.

Heinrich had come intoxicated, and took Petra. He walked to the train station and went home to Fichtelberg. I was mad.

"Why did you let him take the baby?" I cried.

She said "There is no room here for you and a baby and you don't have a place to live and take care of Petra if you have to get a job".

Two days later Heinrich was back again, drunk and demanded, "You must come back with me. You belong with me." He placed a knife to his throat and threatened to stab himself if I didn't leave with him.

I told him, "Go ahead and kill yourself." When he saw that I didn't care, he put the knife down. He said "I'll kill you if I ever see you on the street with a man."

Grandma and I believed him for he had beaten me and choked me in the past.

After Grandma Maria told him to leave, she told me "You must leave town the next day. You will not be safe from him here."

Taking only a few clothes, I left on the train to Nürnberg where I knew some people. They were very nice and got me a job at their neighbor's saw mill and let me work as their housemaid. I did their shopping and cleaning. After about a month, Mrs. Schneider sent me to the butcher. When I came back to the Schneider's house, Mrs. Schneider met me in the hallway. She said, "Bruni, your husband was here looking for you. I told him you didn't work here any longer." She said he was intoxicated. How I didn't run into Heinrich in the street, I do not know.

After I got over the shock, I talked to Mrs. Schneider. "I need to leave and go to another city." She and her husband were very understanding. I had my paychecks. I didn't spend any money while I worked there.

I took a train out of town looking over my shoulder. I was afraid of Heinz and I could not go back to him even if I had to leave Petra. I received too many beatings from him and my mother and her boyfriend. I saw my *Vater* drunk too often at the train station when he was with women. I hated drunken people and was always intimidated by them.

I had left Heinz once before and he sent his mother to my

grandmother's house to bring me back. He told his mother "I'll cut my wrist if you don't go and bring Bruni back."

So I went back with her that time. On the way to her house, she said, "Heinz is waiting for you, happy to see you come back"

He was gone and didn't come home until four in the morning. He went to a dance in the other town. His mother was such a fool, she believed everything he told her. When I told her, "He hit me many times."

She asked me "What did you do to him?"

I replied "He accused me of sleeping with Joseph." My mother-in-law's boyfriend was a man in his early fifties. That woke her up and she told Heinz off. He denied saying it.

I left Nürnberg. I rode to Bad Kissingen, about one hundred kilometers from Nürnberg. I didn't know where I was going and that's where I landed.

This city was and is beautiful and clean. Most houses were white and all built of stone. Fountains and flowers were everywhere and a beautiful rose garden sat in the middle of town. Minerals came out of the ground and people came from everywhere to the Sanatoriums to recuperate. Even Queen Soraya from Persia (Iran) came every year. There is a gambling casino and a beautiful promenade with stores, where only the rich can shop, and ballrooms where you could go to dance every evening. One band would go on break and another would start playing. The food and drinks were out of this world.

I got a room at a bed and breakfast that night. The next morning I went to the employment office for a job. I was advised to work as a housemaid for an American *Armee* officer and his family. They lived up the street by the *Armee Post* in government headquarters. I had a room with a bathroom in the building where housemaids stayed.

Kaptain Van Hook and his wife had four little girls. Two were twins. It was hard for me, for the twins were only a year old and reminded of my baby Petra. I cried almost every night. I also was very hungry because Mrs. Van Hook never cooked enough. All of the girls were skinny. I guess she believed in dieting. She also went to the officer's club every afternoon. I was lucky that Mrs. Van Hook was German, from *München*. She had been to the States with her husband and they were stationed in other places before here. I could communicate with her.

I worked there about a month when one of the maids asked me if I wanted to go to a restaurant and dance hall for a drink. There, we were talking and watching young couples dance when a young fellow, kind of short with black hair and baggy pants asked me to dance. He was an American soldier. I couldn't speak English but he was clever in communicating with me.

As the soldier and I were dancing and talking for awhile, I found out his name, Jerry Rubin and he was Jewish. He enlisted in the Army because he wanted to go to college and become a lawyer. Years later he was a hippy with Abby Hoffman and Tom Hayden who married Jane Fonda. Jerry was a very nice guy and nice to me. He later walked with me to the government headquarters for he had to also go to the Post. He was very gentlemanly and kissed my hand. He asked if we could go out sometime, so we did the next weekend. He was a gate guard working at the gate where the officers entered the Post.

One day Mrs. Van Hook asked me to ride to the Post with her. Had I known what would happen to me and how my life would change again, I would have run without looking back.

As we drove to the gate we had to stop for the guard had to check the car and passengers. A tall blond soldier with the bluest eyes bent into the passenger's window. His face was very close to mine and he looked into my eyes. I do not know what came over me. I had a very overwhelming feeling. I fell in love. Unbelievable but true! Mrs. Van Hook must have noticed that I acted differently. She said "Bruni, stay away from those G.I.s. They are no good and only looking to have a good time."

The next day Mrs. Van Hook went out again. It was afternoon, the children were taking a nap and I was ironing. I could see the back gate to the Post from the living room window. The soldier with the blue eyes could see our house. He saw Mrs. Van Hook leave. The phone rang and it was him. He said something like "Hello". I didn't understand very much but he said in broken German "You are not to go out with Jerry Rubin. You are going out with me." I laughed and hung up the phone.

Jerry called and we went out a few days later. He took me to another couple's house to meet them. They lived down the street. As we walked into the apartment, there was the tall, blond, blue-eyed stranger.

The couple was very nice and we became friends. The guys all worked as gate guards and the blond stranger knew that I was going out with Jerry. He moved right in, he told Jerry at work. "You are not to see her again or you will be in trouble." Jerry told me and asked, "What do you want to do?" With tears in his eyes, he told me, "I cannot marry a Gentile. I have to marry a Jewish girl."

I said, "We can still be friends, can't we?" So Jerry and the couple asked me to go bowling with them one day. They invited YJ Gunter, the blond blue eyes. We bowled and ate at the snack bar. I ate my first hamburger and banana split. YJ was very attentive, but I didn't know that was all show. Several years later I got to know his real character and personality. I was nineteen.

That year I had to have my appendix out and I was in the hospital for a week. YJ came to visit me. My condition made Mrs. Van Hook mad, like it was my fault. She was mean, so I quit working for the captain's family.

I got a room with a girl friend I'd met a few weeks before. I started a waitress job in a restaurant and I was dating YJ Gunter. I was learning English from comic books he brought me. It was not long after we met when Gunter bought me an engagement ring. "I want to marry you as soon as you get a divorce from Heinz. We would pick up Petra and raise her as soon as we marry."

I wrote to my mother-in-law and told her of my plans. She replied and begged, "Please do not take the baby from me. I love Petra."

Heinz knew where I was. He showed up at my rooming house. I told my landlady not to let him in. "She's moved," she told him.

Several months later my divorce was almost final when I received a letter from an insurance company requesting hospital payment. It stated that my husband Heinz came home drunk and attacked his mother with an ax. They put him into a mental hospital and I should pay the bill. My attorney wrote a letter and explained that I never asked for alimony and did not expect him to pay my bills.

YJ re-enlisted to stay in Germany while background checks were made for us to marry. There were physical exams and criminal investigations. Even though my *Vater* and I hadn't seen each other for years, my *Vater* was brought to court to give his permission for me to marry. "I hate Americans and won't give permission," he said.

"How much does this American make?" When the judge heard this he overruled his statements and forced my father's consent. Because of my *Vater's* first refusal, time was wasted. I was pregnant when YJ and I finally married.

Gunter and I went to city hall to marry. Only a few friends went with us as well as a lady who translated all of the papers and the ceremony. YJ could understand little German. We didn't have any money. We couldn't go out to eat and celebrate. Our friends didn't have much either, but when you are young and in love, those things don't matter.

Sadly poverty followed me all through my marriage. My husband spent all the extra money we had. He started going out alone.

At twenty-two, I was pregnant two times in two years. Susi was born in 1961 and Peggy Sue in 1962. There was no money for babysitters. We got an apartment when we married and I was very busy with the little girls. I had no dishwasher or a washing machine. I did all the laundry in the bathtub and hung the wash on the line. We had no car. I did the grocery shopping with both of the babies in the buggy. We went home by taxi—folded baby buggy, babies, groceries and me.

Six months pregnant with Peggy, I wanted to go to the *Amerikan* movie to see "Gone With the Wind" in English. YJ did not want to go with Suzi and me. I asked Doris to go with me. The movie lasted over three hours. As we came to the exit, I saw my husband standing there. He did not say one word. We all walked home together. Doris went to her place and I walked into our apartment not suspecting a thing. I sat Suzi in her playpen. Suddenly I saw stars and felt terrible pain on the side of my face. He'd slapped me. My ear was ringing. Startled, I looked at YJ.

He looked angry and said, "You bitch. You better not ever sit beside a nigger again." I was stunned. I didn't ask why I couldn't sit beside a black man in the movie. I was afraid to ask. I cried. My abdomen hurt and I ran toward the door. YJ came after me and pushed me through the door. Without a coat, I stood outside for at least an hour in the cold and snow. I begged him to let me in. He finally opened the door. That was the first time he hit me.

When I was still pregnant with Peggy, I soon heard that he was seen with this German girl or that German girl and even some of my girlfriends were sleeping with him. YJ told me "I am too young to be married." Once I confronted one of those girls. When YJ heard about it he beat me and warned me never to talk to his girlfriends again. I couldn't comprehend what happened to me. It was like a bad dream. When he hit me and I begged, "Please don't hit me again." He hit me more. Another time I brought a girl in front of him to tell him she had sex with him. He looked at this girl with a very threatening demeanor. She was afraid and denied it, telling me that she had not been seeing him. I was obviously pregnant at that time, too.

In Germany, for Peggy's birth, I rode in the ambulance to the Army hospital alone. YJ claimed he needed to take care of Susi. Yet he left Susi alone in the apartment. Heidi, a cousin of my landlady, finally went upstairs to take care of Susi and watched her while YJ went out running around the bars.

When YJ got home at four in the morning, he slipped into the babysitter's bed. Heidi was only fifteen-years-old and sleeping at our house while watching Susi. I heard about it when I came home from the hospital. He threatened to kill Heidi if she told me. She told me the truth when I confronted her in his presence. He choked her and I had difficulty stopping him. Finally he let go. She thought he would divorce me and marry her. It all was a horrible nightmare.

Earlier that night, Heidi and I went to a party by taxi where my husband had gone. When we walked in the door, I saw a blond girl fly off YJ's lap. I was outraged. I just had his baby three days ago and here he was with another woman. I went up to him and back-handed him six times. He did not move. All was quiet in the room. I walked out crying. Heidi followed. That morning around three, he knocked the door in and hollered, "You hit me at the party. Now I'll let you have it." He beat me about the face four times.

Suddenly YJ got orders to go back to the States and I had to go with him right away. We came to the United States on an Army ship. Peggy Sue, named by YJ from Buddy Holly's song, was only six months old when we got the news. I asked YJ, "When are we going to my hometown to pick up my little girl, Petra?"

He told me, "I am not interested in raising another man's child and can not afford to feed another mouth." Slowly I realized the sacrifice I'd made, yet I knew that it would be best not to subject this little girl to a stepfather who was mean and never even looked at his own babies. He held Peggy for the first time when she was eight months old.

When I refused to come to the United States with him, he got on his knees "I love you. You must forgive me." I had forgiven him many times already. I loved him with all my heart and believed he would change. I hoped he would love me.

With a heavy heart, I decided not to take Petra to another country where everything was uncertain. I wrote to my mother-in-law Maria that I would sign custody papers. The court decided that only my mother-in-law could raise my daughter. Heinz should only have visitation privileges. The saddest and hardest thing for me was that I had no money and no time to travel one hundred and fifty kilometers to see Petra one last time.

I also was terribly afraid of Heinz. YJ was not supporting me in this predicament. He was equally as mean as my ex-husband. I often remembered what Mrs. Van Hook told me as we were in the car "Stay away from the soldiers". I did meet a few nice guys on the *Armee Post* and at the restaurant. They also warned me to stay away from Gunter as he is a "hillbilly".

I asked what a hillbilly is. They laughed at me and said "A hillbilly is someone who keeps his wife pregnant in summer and barefoot in winter. They eat nothing but beans and potatoes. They have no shoes." I didn't know what they meant.

While we were dating YJ was very nice and attentive. I suppose it was all an act. I guess he also knew that I would stop seeing him. At that time I had no reason to tolerate bad treatment from him. I could have dated someone else, even a German.

As September 1963 came near, I went back to the restaurant to work. We didn't have suitcases to pack our clothes in. YJ didn't make an effort to give me money or earn extra money. My ex-boss let me work for two months. Around September sixth or seventh we took a cab to the train station outside of town.

From Bad Kissingen to Bremenhaven we rode an Express train all day and all night at one hundred and fifty kilometers per hour. We had a sleeping compartment all night. It was very elegant. The train had a dining car. I kept asking "How much longer?" We finally arrived at ten the next morning and took a cab to the dock where the *Armee* ship "UPCHAIR" was waiting.

We had a cabin with two bunk beds assigned to us. Many soldiers and many *Armee* families were on the ship. The dining room and the food were "out of this world". Only after one day at sea, I got seasick and could not eat. Yet we had to report to the dining room daily with our children. We were to dress up daily, no casual clothing. Although I was ill, I had to take care of my babies.

YJ went daily, all day long and played cards with other fellows. He only watched the children when I needed to go to the laundry room to wash clothing. It actually was very nice on the ship. They showed movies and evenings held live entertainment. Soldiers with their wives danced the Limbo or Rock and Roll and the Twist. The upper deck was very cold and windy. After we went to the dining room for breakfast, it was the rule that you stayed on deck. You could not go to your cabin till after lunch.

It was terribly hard for me to entertain and take care of Susi and Peggy while I was so ill. Peggy was still in diapers and Susi was two-years-old and kept running away from me. I was in tears daily trying to balance my self on the rocking deck, change diapers and look at food when I gagged each time.

On September 19, 1963 we finally arrived in New York City. It took hours to get off the ship. We had made friends but we had to leave them just as we had to leave friends in Germany. It was very hard also not being able to say good bye to my sister and her family and my dear grandfather, Simon and my brother, all my cousins and my Aunt Emilie and Uncle Paul. I left the past behind and another chapter of my life began.

It was very frightening and the future seemed so unsure, knowing already that I had no support and understanding from my husband. I kept consoling and praying to myself, still hoping that life with my husband would improve. I hoped that the *Armee* would protect me, knowing that YJ would be in the army for twenty years and we would be living at different countries and different army posts.

In New York/Manhattan we took a taxi and rode to the Greyhound bus station. I could not believe my eyes! I almost laughed out loud as we rode through Manhattan. The tenements looked like "little Italy" on the slums! Black people looked unclean on the streets. They had no shoelaces in their shoes. Wash was hanging on lines across the streets, connected from one house to another tangling across the street high above us. It was all so noisy and very dirty. Hundreds of people ran or walked hurrying along. I knew for sure that I didn't want to be there. I wanted to turn and go back home.

We finally boarded the bus. I was thinking that we didn't have to go far, but we rode all afternoon and all night with two wiggling babies. I asked YJ "When are we going to be there?" He said "Soon." In Baltimore, Maryland we traveled at night through the city on a certain street. It was a route or something. Blacks were out on the sidewalks in the street drinking and hollering, sitting and standing in front of their houses on the grass, raising hell. The doors and windows in the houses were wide open, because of the heat, I guess. I did not see any furniture in those rooms, everything looked so empty. Maybe they were too poor to have furniture or curtains.

So far, I did not have a good impression of *Amerika*, the land I heard so much about. I felt like I was on another planet. It was good that I was young and naïve for I still didn't know what lay ahead of me. I was in for a rude awakening which lasted the next thirty years. I looked forward to seeing the in-laws house and to meet my husband's family.

I knew he had a large family with ten siblings. He told me they were poor. It did not matter to me. I was thinking that we would only visit and live in Columbus, Georgia for a few years, where my husband would be transferred. He never told me he had to be at Ft. Benning, Georgia in training to fly and jump out of helicopters in Vietnam. I had no idea that he would be in Vietnam two years later. He was to mark out the targets that they were going to blow up on the ground.

At the Greyhound bus station the next morning, September 20 in Tennessee, I said, "I should change my clothes and change the children."

YJ said "Not necessary, my folks won't care".

"Well, I'm changing the children and myself." I wanted to make a good impression. In the restroom of the bus station, I washed my babies and myself and we changed our clothes.

We hailed a cab. With three suitcases and two children, we rode about twenty miles. We drove towards the Smoky Mountains on the highway. I could see the mountains in the distance. Then we rode onto a dirt road only about ten feet wide. The grass grew six feet tall on each side. I noticed some kids' heads above the grass, moving and following the cab. I asked, "Who are they?"

YJ said, "My brothers and sisters."

Suddenly we stopped after riding about a mile on that road.

I saw a shack with rags stuffed in the windows. There were no stairs, the shack was sitting on blocks. YJ said, "We're here!"

I looked dumb and asked, "Where?"

He said, "Here".

I asked several more times, "Where's the house?"

YJ said kind of embarrassed and impatient. "Here" he said pointing to the shack.

It hit me. A light went on in my head. The kids surrounded the taxi. My husband's brothers and sisters were dirty and unkempt. I felt sorry for them. They were all under seventeen down to two.

We finally got out. YJ talked to his siblings and told them who I was. We climbed into the shack.

I knew what hillbilly meant and what the soldiers were telling me.

Susi sitting on cart as the Gunters arrived in America.
Bruni, YJ and girls traveled by bus from Manhattan to live
with his family in the hills of Tennessee. September 1963

Chapter Twelve

1962-1964
New Jersey and Pennsylvania

While the world endured the Cuban Missile crisis, and the Civil Rights Act was signed, Peggy began her career and marriage.

Two summers, I left my job at Chautauqua Lake early and I traveled with my cousin, Patty and her husband Ralph as a babysitter for their two children. Ralph's family had rented a large house at Atlantic City, New Jersey. My neighborhood girlfriend, Joyce, went with me as my companion and helper with the children. We watched baby Carrie, and toddler David and sometimes other family children. The house was near the Boardwalk and we walked the children daily up and down the famous walkway. At that time, it was not as commercialized as in later years, only a boarded walk above the beach lined with interesting shops. We also took the children to the beach. Joyce and I rented bikes and rode around town and the boardwalk area. I was dating Bill at the time and one of his college buddies lived nearby. Joyce and I would meet him on our days off. Willy showed us the area and told us of life in the dorms with Bill. "Remember how we confused you with answering the dorm phone with Joe's Pool Hall. Eight Ball speaking. Who in the hall do you want?"

I nodded. "For awhile I never knew if I had the right number. You would always answer with silly lines. I fell for it every time."

The following summer with Pat and Ralph, Joyce and I babysat for then toddler Carrie and preschooler David at Cape Cod. We stayed in a rented cabin at the Cape. I kept a list of places my cousins went and liked.

My last summer at Chautauqua, Bill came to drive me home. My dad was having major surgery. I was glad to see Bill but I burst into tears when I saw him. The tiredness of working all summer, worry about my dad's condition and stress of making arrangements for Bill's rescuing me overwhelmed me. My crying scared both of us. Sitting in Bill's car on that hot summer afternoon, I laid my head on his chest and soaked his shirt with my tears. He just held me. Crying was a good release, but embarrassing as I saw myself as a strong person. I knew then I could trust Bill with my heart. I loved him.

***

I graduated from Grove City College in 1962, at twenty-one, with a degree in Elementary Education and a minor in French. I was qualified to teach grades K-12 and French. I was a teacher! My advisor encouraged me to go to graduate school and knowing I was going back home, suggested the University of Pittsburgh.

It was hard to say goodbye to friends I had made over four years at Grove City and know we might never see each other again. We made tearful promises to keep in touch. Some of us would see each other at weddings that summer. I took my first long bus trip alone from Pittsburgh to the middle of Pennsylvania for my friend, Margey's wedding and on to be Maid of Honor at my roommate Betty Ann's wedding. My parents met me in Betty Ann's hometown for the wedding. From there, they were driving on to Edinboro Lake again for vacation. I rode back to Pittsburgh with a friend, stayed overnight at my cousin Patty and Ralph's. The next morning Bill met me, drove us to his grandfather's funeral, then onto Edinboro and vacation with our parents.

I was feeling very mature for making all my travel arrangements and getting where I was supposed to be during those two weeks. The stress caught up with me after Betty Ann's wedding. As I waved good-bye to the newly-weds, I fell sobbing into Betty Ann's mother's arms. Betty Ann and I had shared a lot in our college and Chautauqua years together. Now we were on our own.

My tears surprised me again as I vowed that it would take a lot to make me cry as my high-strung mother cried easily. It bothered my dad and me to see her dissolve into tears. We tended to leave her alone at those times. I realize now, that they were tears of a perfectionist's frustration, tears of a migraine sufferer's pain and tears of a proper Scotch- Irish Presbyterian woman's discomfort living amid a loud, fun-loving German Catholic family.

I returned to my hometown, lived with my parents, and accepted a teaching job in Hopewell-Independence-Raccoon Township School District outside of Aliquippa. I bought a car, a brand new four door aqua Chevy II. I would proudly announce to all, "I am a big girl with a big girl job and big girl pay." Suddenly I was responsible for loan payments and car maintenance. Proudly, I paid off the car loan in two years and drove it three more years. I became a responsible citizen at the same time when my dad took me to register to vote.

I became a first grade teacher in Raccoon Elementary School in Hopewell Township outside of Aliquippa. I was assigned to the classroom next door to my friend, Elaine! Ironically, Mother took me to visit my first grade teacher before I started teaching! Mrs. Henry had retired and talked to me about first graders. She didn't scare me anymore.

With twenty-five first graders, I learned first grade material. We had fun and worked hard to learn reading, writing, and arithmetic in many different ways. It was exciting to watch little readers and writers develop from my instruction! These children had not had kindergarten and some were very immature. One fell asleep every afternoon, others wet their pants. Then I would call the janitor to clean up and I'd take the children for a walk around the halls. "Puff the Magic Dragon" was a popular song at the time. Elaine and I would play the song on the one record player we had. It sat in the halls between the two rooms. The children loved the song and looked forward to listening to it at quiet time.

As a first year teacher, it really hurt to face some parents and say "Your child is not ready for second grade." I had conferred with my principal and had her backing, but I was presenting this information on my own. The situation was nerve-wracking not covered in student teaching! Yet I knew I was doing the right thing for the children.

I also learned how to give clear directions that year. One day when the children were working at their desks, I said, "When you are finished, turn your crayon boxes over and I'll know you are done." Twenty-five first graders dumped their crayons on the floor and turned over their crayon boxes! That's what I told them to do.

I taught first-graders French on my initiative. We sang songs, learned to count to ten and greeted each other in French. At the end of the year, we presented a play in French to the school and parents. Afterwards, I received a call to start the French program and teach reading at the junior high school.

That same year my friend Wella (Luella) from college was diagnosed with a serious illness. Her mother called and asked me to go to her home in Ohio to convince Wella to go to John Hopkins in Philadelphia for further diagnosis and possible treatment. I spent a weekend with her. Afterwards Wella made the trip, but her illness was too advanced for treatment. A few months later, my mother came and sat on my bed early one morning and held my hands. "Wella's mother just called. Wella died during the night". I was devastated. She was the first of my close friends to die. I asked my mother to write to her family as I could not. Bill drove my mother and me to Ohio and the funeral home. I cried uncontrollably in Bill's arms at seeing my friend in death. We had shared college years and beyond. Ashamed of my outburst, I couldn't go to her parents' house for a present Wella had left for me.

I left elementary school and taught grades 7-8-9 remedial, intermediate and advanced reading and first year French in junior high. I muddled my way though using a language laboratory. Students sat in cubicles with earphones and microphones. Wearing earphones and sitting at a huge console, I could tune into cubicles and speak, hear and tape their responses. In the first days, it was an electronic nightmare! The lab complex had been unused for years. After four years, I could operate it and keep students interested listening to professional tapes while they waited their turn to speak to me, in French, of course.

That first year teaching in junior high school was most embarrassing. A single male teacher and I caught the measles, the only teachers who did! We received endless teasing. We taught at opposite ends of the building and must have taught the same students. As an adult, I was hit hard with the measles. I stayed in bed and slept a lot. I missed a week of school. I talked to Bill on the phone. No visits! I didn't want him to see me.

November 22, 1963, the day President Kennedy died, I was teaching the last period of the day in a one-on-one session with a remedial reading student. The news came over the school's public address system. I was as stunned as everyone in the nation. For days afterwards, I sat glued to the television with my parents trying to understand what and how an assassination could happen in my country.

I was dating Bill regularly. He had graduated from Carnegie Institute of Technology with a Bachelor's degree in Mechanical Engineering and was in graduate school there for a Master's degree in Electrical Engineering. He had graduated as a commissioned officer in the US Army with a deferment from active duty for graduate work.

In the meantime, I started graduate school nearby at the University of Pittsburgh, working in the reading labs and taking courses towards my Pennsylvania Permanent license, Master's Degree and Reading Supervisor's Certification. Those were hot summers in the city with no air-conditioning. My mother's cousin, Audrene, lived in an efficiency apartment in nearby East Liberty. I rented an efficiency apartment in her building. She introduced me to apartment living, cooking for one, and using city transportation. I caught a trolley into the city every morning and evening to and from classes. Standing on trolley islands in June and July heat was as hot as hell. The only breeze was from heated traffic flying by. After morning classes, I would stay on campus, reading for classes, studying for exams and researching assigned topics. Late afternoons, I'd return to my apartment.

Evenings, Bill would walk over from Carnegie Tech and we'd eat one of a variety of dinners I'd learned to cook. I rarely cooked at home as my dad was a big tease. He could always make me mad with his comments. "I could bounce this hamburger off the floor." I refused to cook anything other than macaroni and cheese or spaghetti for him. After dinner in my apartment, Bill would help me with statistics homework, walk back to his dorm, and go out for a late night snack with friends.

Weekends, we met at the Carnegie Museum situated between schools, and caught a trolley into the city then a bus to Aliquippa. At home, we did laundry and visited our parents. We went out Saturday nights and took a bus back to Pittsburgh Sunday evenings. One summer Bill was at ROTC camp. I spent lonely evenings in my apartment sitting at my typewriter by an open window and its cool breeze, typing required papers and wishing we were together.

Bill and I were engaged Christmas Eve 1963. Sitting at Midnight Mass I paid more attention to the light shining off the diamond than the mass. Writing our engagement announcement for the local newspaper, I discovered that my name Margaret Ruth is the reverse of my future mother-in-law's Ruth Margaret. I wondered aloud to Bill if he saw it as a good omen. He never even noticed the connection.

With our school schedules, Bill and I decided on an August wedding for the following summer. We were in love and would make our uncertain future work! Later I learned that he had told his parents that after our first meeting he knew he would marry me. It took me longer to realize I would marry him!

The summer of '64 was tense. I was living at home teaching summer school mornings, going to summer school evenings, planning a wedding and attending bridal showers. Afternoons, I did homework for two classes, ran pre-wedding errands and tried to stay calm. My mother made many of the wedding arrangements. She remodeled my Cousin Patty's wedding gown to fit me, reserved the place for the reception, and filed all the invitation replies.

I was busy with school, but it was MY wedding and I felt left out! I regretted not having the chance to try on other styles of wedding gowns. Mother and I argued. After she had ordered one more thing without asking us, I exploded. "Whose wedding is this?" Shocked, Mother answered "I am only trying to help." We agreed to divide responsibilities. Bill was working in the engineering labs at Tech and tolerated listening to my frustration. He admitted that he was frustrated, too! He had graduated from the Master's Program in Electrical Engineering and, still an officer in the army, been accepted for the doctorate program at Tech. He applied and awaited a second educational deferment or army assignment.

We had planned our wedding for August first. Bill says it was so he could remember the date. We didn't know where we would be after that date. It could be anywhere in the world on army assignment or in the area continuing our educations. Late July Bill received notice of deferment. He could enter the doctorate program. I could continue my job. We could stay in the Pittsburgh area and look for a place to live as husband and wife.

At one of our first Tuesday lunches, Hilde says, "Your childrens' bunk beds are beautiful. Where did you buy them?"

"Bill built them," I say.

"But your husband is a professional, not a builder by trade," she says. "Does he have the tools?"

I nod toward the basement door. "He has a workshop."

"Where did he learn to build furniture?"

"His dad was an engineer and also built things."

"And what else did Mr. Hanna build?"

I rest my elbow on the table and think. "He built the end table speakers, the double bookcase, his desk."

"And what else?"

"He designed and built the boys' double desk where each has room for a chair and drawers."

Hilde looks bewildered. "Why didn't you buy all that furniture?"

Brunhilde's father Ludwig Maurer in his WWII uniform

Brunhilde's mother Elisabeth Maurer 26 years old

Heinrich Johann and Brunhilde's wedding 1958

YJ Gunter on base in
Germany early 1961

Brunhilde at Franklin
Park Conservatory,
Columbus, OH 1990's

Pauline, Austin and Peggy Leis at
Leis grandparent's home 1940's

Peggy with Uncle John's dog 1952

Peggy's college graduation with Mother and Bill 1962

Peg and Bill's wedding 1964

Carefree Peg on vacation 1990's

Chapter Thirteen

1963-1965
Cosby, Tennessee

While Martin Luther King gave the "I Have a Dream" speech, and Kennedy and Malcolm X were assassinated, Bruni experienced life in America.

In the shack in Tennessee, I saw children and an older lady, lots of beds and a sofa, some chests and dressers. And in the middle of the room, a large wood stove. The long room was divided by a wooden wall. There were openings with no doors. The wooden floor had holes. Grass and weeds grew up through them. Sand and dirt covered most of the floor. I passed through the opening and went to the doorway at the back wall. In that large room was a stove and refrigerator, a long table with wooden chairs. A bed stood in the corner. Fleetingly, I observed a wringer washer and a small table with a couple of water buckets on them.

It was hot and I was dazed by what I saw. I never saw anything like it. I opened the back door and went outside, towards a small creek. An outhouse on stilts straddled the creek. I dropped to the ground and sat beside the water. After awhile, my husband came out to find me. I had a very hard time comprehending where I was. My head was spinning. YJ sat beside me and said "I'm sorry. I had no idea they lived like this. When I left five years ago, they lived in a log cabin somewhere up the road."

I managed to spit out, "If the ocean wasn't between here and Germany, I would walk home. I'm homesick already."

YJ said "We're not staying here long, only a month."

I got up and went back into the shack. I wondered where the in-laws were. The older lady there said, "Your mother-in-law, Estelle, is working and would be home later. "I am Belva, her sister." She turned out to be a nice lady. She saw my pain and disappointment. "I don't want to be here either," Belva said. She never married. She had crippled hands and could not work. She floated from one relative to another, stayed here and there for a few months. Sometimes she stayed in Georgia.

Everybody stared at me and my little girls. "They look clean and very pretty," they said. My little babies had blond curly hair and pretty blue eyes. Susi's eyes were greyer. I always kept the girls clean and they looked healthy compared to all of the sloppy looking creatures there.

We sat down and they asked questions. "Where are you from?" Pointing to the little girls they asked, "Do they speak English? How long did it take for you to get here?" I answered all their questions.

Around seven o'clock that evening, Estelle, my mother-in-law came home from work. I liked her right away. She was a little woman and I could tell that she had a perm. Her hair looked clean compared to everyone there. Weeks later, I never saw her wash her hair. The children never washed their hair or their bodies. They never took a bath for they did not have a bathtub or a shower.

Barbara was YJ's fifteen-year-old sister. She cooked potatoes and heated beans and made biscuits. We all sat around the long table and ate and drank water or Kool-Aid. I washed my children's hands and faces and changed Peggy's diaper before we turned in around nine o'clock. In a corner, my husband and I and the little girls squeezed in a double bed under a curtain-less window. My husband said, "Use the outhouse before going to bed, for there are brown bears outside the shack at night." They had several dogs that slept outside. It was a restless night with the four of us sleeping in one bed. In the morning, all the children got up early. Breakfast consisted of biscuits, jelly, black coffee and grits which I did not eat. I never liked grits even years later.

I noticed the boys and girls went to bed wearing their dirty clothes and never changed days later. Estelle went to work again at a motel. Barbara cooked potatoes the same as the day before.

I wrote a few letters after I took care of the babies. "This place is nothing like Germany. The poor here ARE poor! We have nothing." I went outside to walk around. The Smoky Mountains loomed right before my eyes. A large Buick belonging to my father-in-law James drove into the backyard. He came home with Estelle. James had black hair and dark blue eyes. He was very skinny and handsome. He shook my hand. I somehow figured out that he stayed at a sanatorium. He had TB and could not live with the family. "I came to see my son and his new wife from Germany". He looked me up and down and said, "She's beautiful with red hair and so clean looking." He looked at my mother-in-law and his daughters and asked "How come you don't look clean like her?"

Gail, another sister, was very pretty. Barbara was big and had an ugly nose. Another sister, Phyllis, was not pretty. She was skinny and quiet. Sue was two and a half, six months older than my little Susi. She kept pushing my Susi out the door. Susi fell three feet and hurt herself. She was bleeding and later had a scar on her leg. YJ finally stepped in and told Sue not to ever push Susi again.

The first night James was home, we went to bed again at nine. All of the beds were filled with children. Belva slept on the sofa. It was very cold at night in the shack. We were asleep around three when the dogs started barking and running around the shack. YJ woke up. So did James. David, YJ's seventeen-year-old brother, started talking "Who could be coming down the road?" The room lit up, lights shone in the curtain-less windows. Everyone sat up saying "Did you see that light? From another corner came, "What's happening?"

James got out of bed. He had his clothes on like everybody else. Only I wore a nightgown. YJ was in his underwear and a T shirt. I hugged my crying girls close. "What's going on?" I kept asking. The dogs barked so loud. Everyone was talking, "Who's there? Can we go look? This is scary!" James went to the door and reached for the loaded shotgun which was always in the corner by the door.

Cars came to a stop in front of the door and by the side of the shack. Someone was knocking on the door, really banging and shouting, "James Gunter, Internal Revenue. Open the door."

I sat upright in bed. The babies were crying, frightened by a flashlight. I screamed when a face appeared in the window beside us.

About three or four men in trench coats and hats barged into the shack and came to the corner where I sat in bed. "Who are you? Do you know who we are?" I shook my head afraid to speak, afraid to move.

The men looked around at the family. "Quiet all of you. We're here to search this house. Stay where you are." They went to the crawl space in the ceiling up the ladder and looked around up there. I was thinking, "Wow, they look like Frank Sinatra or Humphrey Bogart in those trench coats." I did not know anything about Internal Revenue or FBI. After a few minutes they took James by the arm and led him outside. They pushed him into one of the cars and drove away. "All right everybody, back to bed. The IRS heard about James coming home and came to look for moonshine," YJ said. "They also were looking for Charles."

"Who's Charles?" I asked "He's our brother in prison for armed robbery," someone said and added. "He's good looking and a lady's man." I never met him.

We all tried to go back to sleep. The younger brothers and sisters asked, "Why did they take away Daddy?" the older ones asked, "Why did he let them take him away?"

Early in the morning someone made a fire in the woodstove. We ate biscuits and drank black coffee again. Everyone talked about the previous night. "Did you see how big those men were? They looked like gangsters. They didn't find anything. Why were they here?"

James came back home that morning. They let him out on bail. All day the men and women sat around the stove. Another son, JC came with his wife and three small children. They kept rehashing the incident, chewing tobacco and spitting across the room into a spittoon which sat beside the stove. It amazed me how they aimed and spit into that small bowl. It was disgusting.

I took care of my babies and went out and played with them. Some of the children showed me small red tomatoes on the bushes and we ate them. I was hungry and tired of potatoes and beans and biscuits. YJ went with me and his brother to the store and bought some meat and baby food for little Peggy. After a few weeks we were broke, because our money went for food for the whole family.

A few days later, James went to the sanatorium. The IRS could not put him in jail because of his TB. He would have gone to prison for twenty-five years for making moonshine the last twenty years, but could not be confined because of his illness. Estelle would have gone too, but she had nine children at home.

Larry and Terry were two other sons. They were nice little boys around eleven and thirteen. I kept looking at the very large pile of dirty laundry in the corner about five feet high. I could not stand to look at it. The children had no clean clothes and school was about to start. The children did not go to school for some reason.

I told YJ, "I'm bored and want to wash those clothes." I had swept the dirty floor and washed diapers and hung them out. He heated water over a fire outside in a large tub. I also used that tub to wash myself and my girls. YJ put that tub inside the outhouse where I took a bath in it. He sat outside the outhouse until I was done for the door did not lock. The family all laughed at me "You're wasting water. It's not healthy for you to wash your babies all the time." They stared at me when I brushed mine and the babies' teeth. They never saw a toothbrush before.

When YJ heated the water in the tub over a fire, he carried the hot water in buckets inside the shack and poured it into the wringer washer. We carried numerous buckets from the well to the fire to the washer and washed and rinsed all the dirty clothes. We must have done twenty loads of laundry for three days and hung it on the lines and fence outside. The children watched "What are you doing? You're washing all our clothes. We can't wait to wear them." All three days, they sat on the steps and did not help.

For several weeks I ironed all the clothes on the table. There was no ironing board. Estelle put the clean clothes on the children without washing the children first. They went to school dirty, but finally with clean clothes. I was told that everyone talked about the Gunter children wearing clean clothes.

YJ was actually nice to me and acted like a real husband. Estelle scolded him "I will not approve of you hitting her." She looked up at him. "Better not try it in front of me."

After one month, YJ hitch-hiked to Georgia to report to the army. He had no money. He claimed that the army made a mistake in his pay and he could not pay for rent for an apartment. As soon as he got paid, he would pick up the babies and me.

I waited two months. He had left me there.

YJ posing beside his family's shack in the Smoky Mountains
with Peggy on his shoulders, Susi in front, his brother
and sisters beside them. September 1963

Chapter Fourteen

1964-1969
Pennsylvania, Maryland and Ohio

While race riots and Viet Nam War protests escalated and Neal Armstrong landed on the Moon, Peggy began life as a wife and mother.

On a clear hot August morning in 1964 Bill and I were married in our hometown church. I left from my parent's home in the only air-conditioned car in town on loan to us from the local funeral director. I was calm, but worried about Bill. He was known to pass out in our non air-conditioned church. I carried an ammonia capsule inside my glove.

Betty Ann, my college roommate, stood as Matron of Honor, Joyce, my childhood friend, and my cousin Charlotte, were bridesmaids. It was exciting to finally see the girls carrying white daises and wearing the shimmering gold dresses made by my neighbor, a fashion design student. As my dad and I started down the aisle, I whispered to him not to cry or we both would cry. Friends and family said I was beaming!

I was glad to see the priest who had given us our Pre-Cana (marriage preparation instructions) standing at the altar with Bill, his grad school friends and my cousin Bob. We didn't know until that day which priest would witness our marriage. Bill seemed calm as he took my hand and we were married in the last Latin Nuptial Mass in our church. The ceremony changed into English the next week. My mother knew all her

Protestant friends would be following her responses in the mass. She had written when to sit, stand and kneel on her long blue gloves.

The brunch for the wedding party and reception for relatives and friends was held at the Sewickley Motor Inn, across the river from Aliquippa. We took all formal pictures of bridal party and families in the reception room as it was too hot outside. In the receiving line, I was excited and happy to meet all who had come to celebrate with us. I was relieved, too that all the wedding plans had gone well. One photo shows me standing in the reception line without my shoes. When it was time to change into our traveling clothes, I couldn't believe we were married and would change in the same room where my friends were with me. I sent my cousin Charlotte to give Bill his traveling clothes to change in the men's room!

We were sent off amid a shower of rose petals and rice and had to stop on the turnpike and vacuum the swirling petals and piles of rice out of the car. We had a quiet dinner in a nice restaurant near the motel where we stayed as husband and wife. I called my parents and heard their party in the background. They were celebrating, too.

Bill and I tried not to look like newlyweds. We poured the rice our families and friends had put in our suitcases into a wastebasket in the room. It had a hole. Rice spread out over the carpet! We could only laugh and be thankful for our sense of humor which would save us many times in our marriage.

For our honeymoon, we drove to Cape Cod and visited the places my cousins, Patty and Ralph, had gone when I babysat there for them years before. We enjoyed the beautiful part of the country with antique shops, sand dunes, and long stretches of ocean views, an entirely different world from the hills of Pennsylvania. We could relax after the tensions of the summer and just be together.

When we returned home, we found a sticker on the back of the rearview mirror saying "Just Married". Then we knew how everyone knew to congratulate us wherever we went. We didn't think we looked like newlyweds.

We'd rented an apartment in Sewickley where we could see trains on railroad tracks along both sides of the Ohio River, and beyond the hills on the far side, planes approaching the Pittsburgh Airport. Our apartment was located between Hopewell Township where I taught and

Pittsburgh where Bill attended grad school and worked part-time in the engineering labs. Each weekday morning, we would kiss in the parking lot, leave in our separate cars and head in opposite directions.

Lying in bed the first night back from our honeymoon, we were startled by a brilliant light lighting up the whole room. We grabbed each other and sat up in bed. Were we being filmed? Was the apartment on fire? Were the police after us? The loudest "HONKS" from a fog horn followed. Terrified, we rushed to the window to see a tugboat with its revolving search light lighting up the area. The tugboat and its barges were approaching the locks and dam further up the river and were announcing their approach. We didn't know we lived along the signaling waterway. When it happened many more times, we were prepared. What a welcome to our new home!

Bill and I were finally together everyday and living the life we'd planned. Our third floor apartment had a kitchen, living/dining room, two bedrooms and a bath. I would come home from teaching start dinner, relax, and wait Bill's return from Pittsburgh. One evening as he came up the walk to our building, he looked up to see me leaning out the kitchen window yelling, "They're on fire!" He rushed up the steps to see our small toaster oven filling the small kitchen with smoke from burning pork chops. Bill unplugged the oven and doused it with baking soda. There were many meals I never repeated that first year, Bill's approval of disapproval of a meal came in his response, "You could cook this again, or "Don't bother making this again." He told me not to bake "meet pies". I thought he meant meat pies, pies filled with meat, but he meant fruit pies where the top and bottom meet because they are not totally filled.

Not only did we see trains outside our apartment, but inside, too. Bill is a model railroader. Breaking up his train layout at his family home upset him as much as leaving home. He built a layout that fit under our bed in our first apartment. I didn't mind having trains in our home. I grew up with my dad's trains. Bill and I heard trains everyday and nighttimes, enjoyed watching the lighted windows of nighttime passenger trains reflected in the river beyond the parking lot. Throughout our married life, trains would play a big part. Bill ended any comment I'd make about unusual things I did with "That's nothing. I play with toy trains."

Our first years were busy ones. Nights when Bill had classes, I ate dinner with my parents. Nights when I bowled with a teacher's bowling league, Bill had dinner with his parents. As only children, it was hard for each of us to break away from seeing our parents. Weekends we caught up on our household chores, studied, wrote and corrected papers and met with friends.

We invited our parents on New Year's Day for our first family dinner of pork and sauerkraut for good luck in the New Year. Even then, we could never get our parents to admit that they had "arranged" for us to meet that summer at Edinboro Lake.

***

Professionally/formally, known as Margaret Leis Hanna, informally I became Peg Hanna. As a grown up, I chose not to be called Peggy. Peg Hanna sounded better.

Being called Mrs. Hanna was an adjustment. Mrs. Hanna was Bill's mom! Many times, I had to remind myself of my new name and adopt a new signature, using my maiden name as a middle name. Both names gave me the feeling of authority.

My years teaching grades 7-8-9 reading and French were interesting. I loved teaching and learned to understand teens in their turbulent years. One day I heard screaming from a girls' bathroom. I charged in to quell girls' screams and remained to tend to blood gushing from a gash in one girl's arm. She had punched a hole in the glass door, angry about a "breakup" with her boyfriend. I used my school teacher voice to clear the room and sent for the nurse. Then I calmed the terrified teen and myself.

Creating lessons for five classes of students per day and traveling to three different rooms presented a taxing physical challenge. I lugged my materials with me. I was teaching remedial, developmental and advanced reading classes and first year French. My principal was very understanding, especially when I forgot to order a set of books for the next year. As all teachers do, I wondered daily, "Am I helping students?" Teachers were encouraging, but there were days when I leaned against the reading classroom door at the end of the day and wondered, "Is anyone learning here?" Many days I drove home with a migraine headache from the tension of trying to do all that was expected.

Yet there were times when students responded to lessons and seemed to enjoy my classes. Then the work and the worries were rewarded. Every Monday I would read aloud a chapter from a school library book. "What happened in the rest of the book?" students would ask. I'd grin and suggest they check out the book. In a remedial class, I found the incentive for a fifteen-year-old to read on a higher level. He had given up trying. I remembered that he would be old enough to learn to drive the next year. We used the driver's test manual for instruction. We were both excited when he worked hard and learned to read it. I never knew if he passed his test, but he knew the information. Another student in the same class loved to play chess. I didn't know the game. I helped him read the instructions and teach me.

***

In 1967, Bill graduated with a PhD. in Mechanical Engineering, with the distinction of being one of a few to earn the degree at twenty-five. Earlier, he had also been commissioned as a second lieutenant in the US Army. Meanwhile, I had been going to University of Pittsburgh to complete my Masters in Education. When Bill graduated, we had a big party to celebrate and say good-bye to our family and friends. His orders were to report to Officer's Orientation School at Aberdeen Proving Grounds in Maryland. I would end my five years of teaching and graduate classes to go with him.

We rented off base, finding a retired Georgetown University professor's summer home in Maryland at the head of Chesapeake Bay. We shared the beautiful home on the water with another married couple we knew from Carnegie Tech. Patty was from California. Gus was from Pittsburgh and assigned there also. They introduced us to drinking wine and eating spicy foods while we taught them how to enjoy pot roasts and bake pies. The four of us had fun times in that house, entertaining couples from base, learning to live with rusty water, wasps and a box turtle. Patty and I would take shopping trips into Baltimore and Philadelphia. I wrote weekly letters to my parents about army life.

It was hard for Patty and me to adjust to the formality due our husband's rank. I was glad for the set rules, to know exactly what was expected. Patty resented them. We all followed rules set in the men's

Officer's Training Guide. One time Patty and I were invited to one officer's wives tea where I was asked to pour tea and the lid fell off the teapot and splashed into a cup. I silenced the room when I swore! Red faced, I apologized to the hostess. Working so hard to follow all the rules, I thought for sure Bill would be demoted because of my inappropriate behavior.

At graduation in 1967, Bill and Gus were assigned to National Aeronautic and Space Administration laboratories. The thirteen PhDs in their unit were assigned to NASA installations around the nation. All other officers were ordered to Vietnam. We teased Bill and Gus that their country wanted their brains, not their brawn.

Bill was assigned to NASA Lewis Research Center in Cleveland, now known as John Glenn Research Center. Gus was assigned to NASA Ames, a California installation. The four of us parted and went our separate ways vowing to meet again.

Bill and I suspected that I was pregnant. Patty was a nurse and agreed. Bill and I were ecstatic! We were going to be parents! I did not have morning sickness, but became very tired in summer's heat. Leaving Maryland and driving north, it seemed Bill and I stopped at every gas station. Bill would say, "But we don't need to stop for gas!" I would reply, "But I need to pee!"

On the way to the Cleveland assignment we stopped in Aliquippa, confirmed my pregnancy with our family doctor, and announced it to our parents. Bill and I bought champagne and served it in my mother's crystal stemware. I thought lightening would strike as the glasses had held nothing stronger than sherbet in my lifetime! Both sets of parents were present to toast a first grandchild and send us off to Ohio with their blessings.

We rented a town house apartment in North Olmsted, Ohio a suburb near Cleveland Hopkins Airport and Lewis Research Center. With no army base in Cleveland, we could live in civilian housing. Fort Hayes in Columbus, Ohio, was the nearest army facility. At that time, it was only an administrative center. The Cleveland army community was welcoming and helpful to a first-time pregnant couple with references to an obstetrician, advice and lending baby equipment. Bill and I enjoyed our two years there. He built a train layout in our family room and I was schedule-free to read all the books I never had time to read. I knew after baby my reading time would be limited. The library, within walking distance, helped me physically and mentally to wait for baby.

These were times of race riots in the east side of Cleveland. We lived on the west side. People were buying guns in fear of the riots spilling over into the west side. We heard about the riots daily and watched them on TV. Racial prejudice was hard for us to understand as we had grown up among many races in our hometown. We came to understand that what we were seeing was the blacks' frustration at not being accepted everywhere.

After an easy pregnancy, our first son, Lee, was born at Fairview General Hospital in Cleveland. There was no army hospital nearby. I had not gone into labor on his due date and was induced. I started throwing up. The nurses saw this as unusual and the doctor was called. I was sedated and woke up eight hours later when Lee was being born. I couldn't believe I had produced this beautiful almost nine pound boy. I had a son! I was a mother!

Lee was named in the Hanna family tradition. When learning I was pregnant, my mother-in-law stated "There have been Williams with the mother's maiden name in the Hanna family for over one hundred years." She said no more. Lee is William Leis Hanna. We already had a Bill in the family and didn't need another. This boy would be Lee and someone would have to break my arm to know his first name. With all my experience with children, I wondered many times, if I would be a good mother. Would I know what to do with an infant? Breast feed or bottle? What if the baby were colicky? We got along fine. I breast-fed and Lee wasn't colicky.

At my six weeks check-up I asked the doctor why I threw up when in labor. "When you were little, did you throw up when you were excited?" I nodded. He smiled. "You were too excited."

When Lee was about a year old, he stayed at home with two grandmas. Bill and I went to California for a job interview, to visit Patty and Gus there and onto Hawaii to visit Joyce and her husband. Back in Cleveland, Lee wore out the two grandmas. They were not used to chasing a toddler.

After a two-year commitment in Cleveland, Bill ended his military obligation at Fort Knox, Kentucky. Fort Hayes, the army base in Ohio, was no longer in operation. Bill interviewed many places in the spring of 1969. Lee thought Sunday nights were to be spent in his stroller at the airport waving at Daddy boarding a plane. After months of searching, Bill accepted a research position with the first company he interviewed. We moved in August 1969 to Columbus, Ohio where he started at Battelle Memorial Institute, a not-for-profit research center. Our new life began.

Hilde unpacks her sandwich. "What did you bake this weekend?"

She always teases me about baking on the weekends.

"A pie," I say sitting across from her. "There's some left."

"What kind?'

"Always a fruit pie," I say.

"No meet pie where top meets the bottom?"

I laugh. "I can't believe you remember Bill's request. You know who else remembers?"

Hilde unfolds her napkin. "Who else?"

"When the boys grown friends are in town, they stop in and ask if I'm still baking pies on weekends."

"What about Kristin's friends?"

"They remember my brownies. Our exchange students didn't know brownies. They learned to love them, too." I stare out the window as if remembering their first tastes.

Hilde nods. "I didn't know brownies until I came to America."

Mrs. Hanna (Peg) leading reading class in quick word
recognition activity with tachistoscope 1966

Chapter Fifteen

1963-1966
Tennessee and Georgia

While Vietnam War escalated, Civil rights March was held in Selma, and Martin Luther King won the Nobel Peace Prize, Bruni lived as an enlisted man's wife.

Every day in Cosby, Tennessee at the base of the Smoky Mountains, living in the shack of my in-laws with ten or twelve other people was unbearable. I had to do something other than washing and ironing, eating potatoes and beans or vegetable soup without meat. My babies ate the same food everyday. Peggy, only a year old, had diaper rash so bad her little bottom bled. I had no cream or ointment to put on and no way to stop the diarrhea.

Daily, I looked toward the narrow road for a car. I waited for my husband to come from Georgia to pick us up like he promised. Things were going from bad to worse. My brother-in-law, seventeen, called me "Nazi, Go back to Germany."

I finally had enough. YJ was not coming. I decided I was going to him. I had no money.

President Kennedy had just been assassinated. YJ's siblings were jumping up and down, hollering, laughing and saying "Goody, Goody, he's dead. They killed him. Goody, Goody." I looked at them with disgust and realized these people I was living with were ignorant. My mother-in-law and her sister were good and decent, but I didn't know about the rest of the children. I made up my mind that I was getting out somehow.

I walked up the road to my husband's aunt's house. She and her husband had a nice home and owned a gas station in another town. They were decent people and so were the other two aunts that lived in that neighborhood. They had nice homes and owned a grocery store and tobacco fields. My father-in-law was the black sheep of the family a moonshiner with a bunch of kids. YJ's aunt invited me in. "I need to leave," I told them. "Could I borrow twenty dollars for bus fare to get to Georgia?" They were very understanding and agreed that I didn't belong there with his people. I needed to go. They gave me the twenty dollars.

Next I walked to the sheriff's house. He lived in a log cabin with his family, a very nice old man. He agreed to take me and my babies to the bus station in the morning. I needed to be ready at four a.m.

That evening in the dark, I washed myself and my babies in the corner of the shack and put everything I had in two suit cases. I dressed my babies in the clothes we traveled in and laid out my clothes, so I wouldn't have to do all at three in the morning. I took the suitcases and my babies to the door when I saw the approaching lights of the sheriff's car. My mother-in-law, Estelle, spoke to me from the dark. "Bruni, don't go. Wait for YJ to come to get you."

"No," I replied "I am leaving. He will never get me, I know."

The sheriff put my babies into the car with my belongings, and we drove up the muddy road towards the highway. Finally we were on the Greyhound bus to Georgia.

It was a long journey. I arrived late in the evening. I think it was three hundred miles to Columbus, Georgia. The bus station was full of soldiers. It was Thanksgiving and they had an extra day off for President Kennedy had died. It was unbelievable. People and soldiers were in an uproar about his assassination.

I had a piece of paper with my husband's name and address at Ft. Benning. I had no idea how to make a phone call or how to put a dime in the pay phone. I approached a soldier and got him to understand that I needed to talk to the man on the piece of paper. Carrying Peggy and with Susi walking beside me, I followed him to a phone. The soldier talked to someone on the phone and handed it to me. I understood that

I was talking to my husband's sergeant. I explained that I came from Tennessee and my husband took me there from Germany. He told me that Gunter went to Montgomery, Alabama and would not be back for two days. He offered to take me to a motel and I could wait there until his return.

I was upset. That bum went to Alabama instead of coming for us. He had bought a car and was driving around to have fun instead of getting an apartment for us.

The sergeant arrived at the station and loaded us into his car. He stopped at a motel and asked the manager if we could stay there. I had an expensive camera that I could leave with him for payment. He said it was not necessary.

I stayed in the motel room with Susi and Peggy. I washed diapers in the sink. After I'd paid for the bus ticket, I had five dollars. The motel owner sent over breakfast every morning. I was touched. I used the money to buy hamburgers in the evening from a place across the street. Two days after I arrived at the motel, the phone rang at seven a.m. It was YJ. Boy, was he mad! He said "What in hell are you doing here? Didn't I tell you to stay in Tennessee until I was ready to get you?"

The sergeant reported to his commanding officer that Gunter had dumped me in Tennessee and now I was here. The commanding officer ordered my husband to find me an apartment and provide food for me and the children or he would be busted and put in the stockade.

YJ was livid when he picked us up. He took us to a nice place he rented. The landlady lived next door with her daughter. I liked living there. YJ never came home for supper. It was always three or four in the morning when he came home. He always lied and said he was on Post playing cards. A few times I walked down to the pay phone on the corner and called the Post. I was told that he was not there.

I had no money for clothing for me and the girls. I went down the street to a Goodwill store and bought little outfits for twenty-five cents for the girls and dresses for fifty cents for me. I took it out of the grocery money. I told YJ that Susi needed shoes. By that time she was three. YJ ignored me.

One day I noticed little sores on Susi and Peggy's bodies. They got larger and larger and started oozing. Soon their little bodies were covered. I showed YJ. Again, he ignored me. I told him he needed to take us to the Post to the hospital. He looked at me and walked away. I could not drive and the hospital was eighteen miles away. I showed the landlady the sores and told her that YJ ignored me.

I also told her that once he told me if I didn't behave he would take my children and send me back to Germany without them. I believed him. I was so naïve. My kind landlady said, "Don't believe him. He cannot do that".

Finally YJ took us to the hospital. The army doctor was appalled at the sight of the sores covering the girls from head to toe. He asked YJ if he could take pictures of the girls for he had never seen any case of impetigo like it. YJ's head got very big and he smiled proudly because the good doctor wanted to take pictures of his little girls. I finally realized what an ignorant human being he was. The doctor stepped out to get a camera.

I looked at YJ "You are so stupid. You don't even know what he's talking about," I said. "You could get in trouble for letting the babies condition get that bad and not taking them to the doctor sooner". He finally understood.

I had no washer. I had to wash all the laundry by hand in the bath tub. I used the drawer from the refrigerator to carry the laundry out to hang on the line. One Sunday I cooked lunch from our small amount of groceries. It was almost ready when YJ said he was going to the corner store for cigarettes. He didn't return. We waited to eat. I didn't see him until three in the morning. He never told me where he was. I was frantic not knowing what happened to him.

I wrote a letter to my German girlfriend Ursula who I knew in Germany. She also married a soldier and moved to Columbus, Ohio. I told her what a life I had. She said hers was not better, but they had a house and urged me to come to Ohio. I decided to do that because I was not going to tolerate the treatment I was getting from YJ.

My neighbor lady took me to the store and bought a pair of shoes for Susi. It was winter in Ohio and Susi could not get on the bus in bare feet. I took the grocery money and bought a ticket to Columbus, Ohio. The landlady took me to the bus station.

When I arrived in Ohio a day later, my girlfriend's husband picked us up. I stayed with them a week. Suddenly YJ showed up. His commanding officer told him to bring me back. He'd received my letter.

I requested to have my allotment check sent to me in Ohio. I was not going back to Georgia. YJ was sorry as usual and said he was not going to mistreat me and the babies and not going to run around anymore. After a few days of his promises, I believed him.

We drove back to Georgia with him. He didn't like the interference from the landlady so we moved. I liked the apartment and the location. Although it was isolated, it did have a playground about a mile away and a "Piggly Wiggly" grocery store and a Goodwill store where I bought clothes. The new apartment was on 3rd Avenue and closer for him to work. A lot of army families lived there in houses built on blocks about two feet off the ground. The old Jewish landlord lived on the same property. The apartment was furnished like the other place. We had no furniture of our own, no dishes and no linens. YJ didn't think it was necessary to have all that.

We were in the apartment the first night when he turned on the lights in the middle of the night. I thought my eyes were playing tricks on me. I blinked several times trying to clear my eyes. No use. The walls and curtains were covered with roaches. I never saw anything like it. On the floor the largest black bugs I ever saw were scurrying around and disappearing under furniture. I felt that I was going into shock. I asked YJ what all those bugs were. He said nonchalantly, "Roaches and water bugs." He turned over and went back to sleep. I was highly upset and I felt the bugs were crawling over me. I kept hearing noises all night while YJ laid there sleeping peacefully.

A few nights later YJ was home early. We went to bed. The girls had to sleep on a sofa. There was only one large bed with a lumpy mattress and not too clean. The walls in that apartment were very dark and I wanted to paint them. The landlord agreed to buy the paint if I would paint them. I heard noises again coming from the kitchen. YJ opened the kitchen door because I always closed it at night. He stepped into the room and I followed him. A noise from above the refrigerator made us look up.

The largest rat, as big as a small dog, looked right at us. I thought I was dreaming. The rat jumped down and YJ jumped onto a chair. A 6'2" man weighing two-hundred-and-twenty pounds was scared of a rat! I realized now why the bread and bananas disappeared over night. Mornings when I got up, the food had disappeared and I could not figure out what had happened. Believe it or not, YJ went about his routine, going to work and staying out late. He did nothing to find another place. He solved the problem by not coming home at night.

He left me with the children alone in this apartment with the roaches and rats. The neighbors told me that there was a hole in the wall behind the stove and the rats traveled from one place to another. The other G.I. families didn't seem to be bothered by the rats. Of course, their husbands were always home at night. It was reassuring to the lady next door. I put my babies into bed with me every night. I had to watch over them, for those wolf-rats eat fingertips and noses off little children. I lay awake at night and listened to the rats roam in the kitchen.

I took matters into my hands and confronted the landlord. He knew about the problem and never took action. A few hours later, a knock came on the door. It was the landlord. He came in carrying a loaf of bread and something else. Rat poison. He walked into the kitchen and started to open the loaf of bread. He placed the slices on the floor around the stove and proceeded to sprinkle the bread slices with the poison. I felt like someone hit me in the head. I shook my head a few times and tried to catch my breath.

Finally I managed to speak. "What are you doing? You can't do that. I have little children here. I can't watch them every minute. They can pick this bread up and eat it!" The landlord gave me a real dumb look. He didn't understand me. He removed the bread pronto. I told him we were moving.

I couldn't understand where all these stupid people came from. The last months I had been in this country, I saw the majority of people ignorant and stupid.

When YJ came home I told him what had happened. I made him move us. He found a small place quickly. It was a bedroom and small kitchen. The landlady who lived next door told me to move because I was evil. I wore a black bra and panties. She saw them hanging on the line. To her, I was evil to wear this kind of underwear.

YJ moved me again to a place on 4th Avenue. He bought a washer and furniture because I refused to do laundry and his work clothes in the bathtub forever. I ironed all the clothes and fatigues on the table. I had no ironing board. We lived in this apartment for about a month. YJ still didn't come home for supper. On the weekends he disappeared, sometimes telling me he was going for cigarettes and never came back until the next morning to change clothes. My landlady's granddaughter told me YJ was at the beach with his buddies.

One day a friend of his came by the house. I was surprised to see him. I invited him in. We talked awhile and he left. He said he wanted to see YJ. The next weekend he came to the house again asking for YJ. He hung around and finally he hinted that YJ had a girlfriend in Alabama. Phoenix City, Alabama was across the bridge from Columbus, Georgia. Phoenix City in 1964 was a very corrupt city. The mayor and all officials, police were into corruption. Negroes were mistreated terribly. Gambling and prostitution was going on.

My husband drove daily to Alabama to see the girl. I finally figured the reason this friend was telling me this. Those soldiers were so awful. They were always out to have a good time, looking for sex. He was thinking if he told me about my husband seeing other women and leaving me alone, I would need comfort from him and one thing would lead to another. I was shocked but I figured it out.

I started watching the odometer in the car. The miles were always three times more than the thirty-six miles it took to get to work and home. When I found a hair roller in the back of the car, I confronted him. He said the odometer was broken and it doubled the miles. I knew better. He also said the hair roller was mine. I reminded him that I never go anywhere with hair rollers in my hair. I never washed my hair in Germany. I always went to a beauty shop. It was totally new for me to wash my hair and roll it myself. I got used to it like a lot of things since I married that scumbag. When I asked him for a dollar to buy a bra, I was told to go braless.

When I knew for sure that he had another woman, I went to court and got a legal separation. He had to move out and give up his car. He had to stay at the army post and two-thirds of his pay, $200 per month, came to me. It was endless, one problem after another.

It was summer in Georgia. The heat was always unbearable. The humidity was horrible. It rained every morning, then the sun came out. It was like a steaming tea kettle, like devil's kitchen in afternoons. One afternoon I dressed my girls and we walked down the avenue. I always took a walk with my little Susi and Peggy. There was an old swing set in the backyard-nothing else. My children never had a toy. Not even for Christmas would he give me money to buy presents for the girls or me. I never asked anymore because he would not give me any. When he lived with us, he took the television and the radio to the pawn shop. He needed spending money. So I lived in the apartment with the rats and roaches and no TV or radio. My little girls and I took lots of walks, window shopping on Main Street or looking for a playground and with no money for ice cream.

One afternoon I walked with them past the house in which the landlady lived next door. There were also rooms for rent. I looked towards the porch for there were lots of people congregating there. They were loud, drinking and playing cards. My husband was there. He did not even come towards his little girls. He just looked at us and kept playing cards. I kept right on going.

The next morning there was a knock on the door. I was not awake yet and the babies were still asleep. I opened the door to see YJ. He picked me up in his arms. It happened so fast, he had no trouble carrying me. He was so tall and strong. He carried me into the bedroom and raped me. I cried and cried because I could not understand the marriage we had of violence, lies and rape. I still loved this man in spite of everything. He said we should get back together. I knew why he came crawling back. He no longer had a car or money. He was on leave and rented a room next door, yet never came over to see me or his girls, except for the sex.

A tall young woman lived next door. I could look into her windows from my bedroom window. I never paid much attention to her. She had two rooms and lived there with a couple of kids. While my husband was staying next door, I happened to look over towards her windows one evening around midnight. The lights were on and there was my husband sitting beside this woman on her bed. Maybe he was drinking. He never realized I could see into this room or he assumed I was already asleep for my place was dark. I could not believe what I saw.

He got up to leave, but the woman went towards him and reached out to him and at the same time turned off the light. I could imagine what transpired. I became enraged. How dare he come over here the day before and have sex with me and be with this woman at night! I was going to prove to him that he could not deny anything this time.

In the past, he always denied having other women when I was accusing him. I marched over there.

I walked through the building, right up to her door and knocked. No one answered. I finally said loudly, "I know you are in there, you SOB. Come out!" She jerked the door open. "You are with my husband." She was raving at me and turned around into the room. YJ was still sitting on the bed. She started screaming and calling me names.

From somewhere she produced a large knife. She started swinging at me and screaming. I just stood there. I didn't care anymore what happened for I could not take that hell anymore. I forgot about my children. I was so tormented about the misery he put me through. I did not come to this country to live this kind of life. I wanted to die.

Finally YJ sprang into action. He realized he would be in trouble with the army if he permitted this woman to injure me or kill me. He started to grab the woman and wrestle the knife away from her. When she realized that he was defending me, she got furious. She lunged at him. He moved backwards several times to avoid a stabbing. Finally he was able to overpower her and took the knife.

He took me by the arm to lead me out of the house. In a daze, I walked with him. We walked to my house and at the door he wanted to come in. I jerked away from him and told him to get lost. I didn't care if he went back to his tramp. I did not see him for weeks. The woman made a big circle around me whenever she saw me.

Behind my back yard was a village of one or two-room houses. They were occupied by Negroes. In 1964 there were no equal rights. Blacks had to go to certain public restrooms ten blocks away. They rode in the back of the bus. Water fountains were for blacks or whites only. The Negroes behind my back yard always got drunk on cheap wine. They raised hell all night. I stayed awake most of the night because I could not lock the windows. I was afraid one of the Negroes would come in the window and what would happen? I did not have to worry. They would not dare bother a white woman or they would be lynched.

I did not know anything about prejudice or discrimination. I never heard of that in Germany.

YJ, the girls and I took a walk one Sunday afternoon. I noticed as we walked on the sidewalk that the groups of Negroes would step down into the gutter when we approached them. I asked YJ why. He said "Because." That answer wasn't enough for me and I asked "Why because?" He said, "Because they are niggers. They better step into the street when I'm a coming. I'm a white man and them are niggers." I was horrified. I never knew that went on in America.

One day some G.I. wives and I were sitting on the porch. A young Negro passed the house next door and smiled at the white woman. She went to a phone and called the police. When they came, she said the Negro flirted with her. They did not question him. They beat him senseless. He was near death. From then on I was very careful and never said anything to anyone about a Negro. The white police were just waiting for a reason to beat or kill a black. I could not comprehend at what evil planet I landed. I suppose it was like the time of WWII with the Nazis and Hitler and the Jews. At about the same time in 1964 the Negroes and Martin Luther King started the march in Selma, Alabama and things slowly changed for the Negroes.

It was not long after our separation that YJ got orders to go to Vietnam. He trained to fly helicopters and jump out of them. Suddenly he decided he wanted to spend as much time as he could with me and the girls. I met several German girls in Columbus on 4th Avenue. Their husbands had to go to Vietnam too. The girlfriends and their husbands and I got along very well. They invited me and my babies to go to a lake. We had fun. YJ never took me anywhere. One evening the German girls, Frieda and Ruth took me to a Roy Orbison concert. I loved him and his music.

One evening I was next door at Frieda's with my girls. YJ was at my place in my bed when we got home. He said he loved me and wanted to be with me. I told him to leave. I had to call the police when he refused to leave. I didn't want to be with him any longer. The police followed him to the bus station to ride to the army base.

The day came when YJ had to leave for Vietnam. I thought it was just a few hundred miles away. I had not idea about the country or that it was a world away.

YJ had cut the dresses up that he bought me when he found out that he could not sleep with me. After he was gone a few months I found out that he deliberately neglected to make out the allotment for my monthly support. I was not receiving a check and could not figure out what happened.

My girlfriends went home to Germany or another state to be with their families to await their husbands' return from Vietnam. Ruth's husband, Bob, was blown up in a helicopter in front of YJ's eyes. Jerry, Frieda's husband was not right in the head when he came back. They had no children and got a divorce.

My landlady kept asking for the rent. I was confused and had no idea why I was not getting a check. One day my landlady's granddaughter had a date with a guy named David. She introduced me. David said he had been stationed in Germany. We talked and I mentioned to him that I hadn't gotten a check from the army. He said he would take me to Fort Benning to speak to someone.

I dressed the girls and he drove us to the base the next day. Red Cross said they could not help me with money, but they would contact the commanding officer. He forced my husband to do the necessary paperwork. I finally received money after four months.

In the four months, I was desperate for food and money. David started to talk about love and marriage. He gave me money so I could live. He wanted me to get a divorce, but I promised YJ I'd wait until he got back from Vietnam. I knew I could not marry David although he was the only man in my life who treated me and my girls with love and kindness.

I decided to move to Columbus, Ohio to be with my girlfriend Ursula. David took me to the Greyhound bus station. He pleaded with me not to go. I felt so sad and helpless. He was standing there with tears rolling down his cheeks as the bus started out of the depot. My girls waved to him and he waved back and threw them kisses.

Hanna's first house on Heil Drive in 1970
where Peg and Bill began raising their family.
As the family grew an addition was built over the garage.

Chapter Sixteen

1969-1970
Gahanna, Ohio

While protestors were shot at Kent State, and the Vietnam War escalated, Peg came to Columbus, Ohio.

My first look at Ohio's state capital came late at night in the summer of '69 in a Holiday Inn that looked like every other Holiday Inn. Bill had accepted a job as a research scientist at Battelle Memorial Institute. A three-day stay had been arranged for our family to stay in a hotel to look for housing in the area. Lee, at sixteen months, was teething and we ordered from room service, drinks for us and "issum" Lee's word for ice cream to help numb his gums. The desk clerk stated that the dining room was closed, but he scrambled to find ice cream at ten at night and received a good tip.

The next day we looked for housing on both sides of the city. At Bill's new boss' suggestion we rented on the east side so Bill would not drive into the sun to or from work. The townhouse we chose at Williamsburg Square in Reynoldsburg sat at the end of a three-sided grassy square. As its first tenants, we were excited to be in a brand new place. We had a basement and two floors, three bedrooms and enclosed patio. Bill set up a workshop in the basement and spent evenings building a color television set from a kit. Lee stood beside him on a chair "hepping".

One day as I was listening to the radio, I heard a report that there were cows on the freeway. A truck of cattle had overturned and cows were wandering on the freeway north of Columbus. I immediately called Bill at work and asked "What kind of town have you brought us to?" We had just come from big cities and never heard of such happenings.

We knew no one in town and made friends with our neighbors and colleagues from Battelle. I was active in the wives newcomers club which was very formal. It reminded me of officer's wife days. Again, I was on my best behavior. I didn't want to jeopardize Bill's new position. Wives poured from silver tea sets, baked and served elaborate desserts, and had instructions for washing the lace tablecloth. Monthly teas welcomed new members and acquainted them with the history of Institute and the city. Some meetings were held in older member's large suburban homes. I wondered if I would be one of those older members someday and impress another young wife.

Battelle had department picnics and families met and played together. On one of our first picnics, an older couple took us on a long walk and talked to us about the need to balance raising a family and Bill's spending long hours on projects at work. We had agreed that I would be a stay-at-home mom. He and I also agreed that he would come home for supper every night and if he had to, he would go back to work later that night. Otherwise he would never see our children.

We met another Battelle couple our ages with three young children. Margie and I became good friends. She helped me adjust to living and shopping in the Columbus area. We spent days together with children, evenings together as couples and holidays together as our families were out of state. One day I stood speechless from Margie's phone call, "We're moving. Steve has accepted a job in Chicago." I felt as if a hot knife sliced through me. I was divided, happy for them, yet saddened by my loss.

The TV show "Sesame Street" started while we lived in the townhouse. Lee and I watched the first episodes and continued watching as part of our daily routine. We would take a walk after doing the laundry in mornings, eat lunch, nap, have a snack, play, and watch TV till Bill came home for supper.

I took afternoon naps when Lee did. He always took off one sock at naptime. When I got him up I would sing, "Diddle, Diddle, Dumplin' my son John one sock off and one sock," and Lee would sing "on." After dinner Bill played with Lee and helped put him to bed.

My parents came out that fall to see our new place. They loved German Village and eating at real German restaurants in the south side of Columbus. They enjoyed playing with Lee, their first grandchild.

For our first Christmas in Columbus, we expected snow and looked to buy a child's sled. We were told "It does not snow enough in Columbus for sleds". There were none in the stores. That Christmas it snowed. Bill built a box sled for Lee from plywood and we pulled him around the neighborhood.

We enjoyed our townhouse for nine months until the building of a freeway started immediately behind us. Heavy machines roared and bright lights shone into our townhouse twenty-four hours. We were reminded of the bright lights the first night in our first apartment.

Just pregnant with Greg, I wasn't sleeping much and the construction noise kept us all awake. We needed to find bigger quarters, a house. We found a grandfatherly realtor and told him what we wanted. He was considerate of our needs and after several Sundays of touring homes on the east side, found us a house in Gahanna, twelve miles east of Columbus. In each house we toured, Lee sat on Bill's shoulders ducking under doorways and chandeliers.

We decided on a four bedroom, two-floor house with a full basement on Heil Drive in Gahanna. One of our criteria for a house was a full basement for Bill, the model railroader, to construct a layout. We asked for a loan from Bill's parents to help with the down payment. Bill and I were both on the phone and heard Dad say "I won't give you that amount." We both gasped when he said, "We would loan you more to help with moving costs." We were surprised, thankful and relieved with the help for our tight budget. My hand shook when I signed a mortgage to be paid off in 1995. I never considered that date in my life and wondered if I'd live that long!!

Bill's parents came the week before we moved and helped us get ready. Dad, just retired, worked at the house all week painting, making electrical and plumbing repairs. Mom helped me caring for Lee and getting things packed at the townhouse. Some days we took Lee to the house, let him run around in empty rooms and take a nap in his new bedroom. Bill worked during the days and would help his dad get the house ready evenings. We were all tired at night and slept well.

We moved into the house in April 1970. Lee had just turned two. He had a measles shot at his two-year checkup and was the one in a thousand who caught the measles. I was petrified! Four months pregnant with Greg, I delayed making the phone call to the obstetrician, afraid that I could catch the measles and affect the baby I was carrying. I had heard that measles in the first months of a pregnancy could cause deafness and blindness in the fetus. Fortunately, I had had both kinds of measles and was told the affects to the baby's development would be during the first trimester. We were safe!

My parents came to see the new house and help us get settled. We had air- conditioning installed, the first in the neighborhood. We were spoiled as our previous homes had air. Pregnant, I couldn't face a hot summer without it. Whole house air conditioning was a new concept to my parent's generation and they were amazed that we could afford its comfort. We bought the air conditioner from the gas company at the cost of $17.87 per month!

We were homeowners responsible for all maintenance and repairs, taxes and mortgage, appearances inside and out and a growing family. Friends teased us about our having the name Hanna and buying a house on Heil Drive in Gahanna. Others questioned our choice of a big house with only one child. We knew we wanted more than one as we are only children and had seen close relationships develop between brothers and sisters. As a former teacher, I had scouted out the school system visiting the neighborhood elementary school and asking neighbors about middle and high schools. I liked what I saw and heard and knew our children would get a good education.

We quickly made friends with the neighbors. There were other children in the neighborhood, some our children's ages and others babysitting age. This was a great help as we became more active in community and church.

Greg was born on August, 8, 1970. Since we married on August 1, in later years he liked to tell all "I was born seven days after my parent's wedding," omitting the six years in between. His was an easy pregnancy and birth. I had gone to the doctor in the morning and he agreed to induce labor that afternoon as I was two weeks past due date.

After one week, I hoped to hasten delivery and jumped down one step to the basement. After two weeks, I jumped down two steps. I finally asked the doctor to induce delivery for the family's mental health. I was miserable and ready.

Labor was induced and Greg came quickly. Bill and I decided on a name on the way to the hospital. We had used both family names in naming Lee, William and Lee for Leis my maiden name. We felt free to use any name. I liked the combination of Gregory Alan, but couldn't give a child the initials of GA (Hanna) living in Gahanna. Greg is Gregory Michael. At two-and-a-half, Lee accepted him well, but got louder and louder each day. He needed attention, too. Our mothers came at separate times to help with babies and housework in the following weeks.

When Lee turned three he started preschool three days a week. At the first parent-teacher conference, the teacher asked me "Is Lee used to structure?'

I nodded. "We go to the basement every morning after breakfast to do laundry and come up for a walk, then eat lunch".

The teacher said, "I can tell. Lee gets very upset when there is any difference in the preschool routine".

Greg napped while Lee was gone. I did as much housework as I could in that time. One day I told Bill that I couldn't keep up with everything. We didn't have a neat house like our mothers did. Bill's response, "I didn't marry you to be like my mother." I loved him more that day. It was then I decided I could keep my house clean or neat, but I couldn't do both.

Mornings when Lee didn't go to preschool, we would be in the basement while I did laundry. Greg would jabber from a playpen. Lee would roll the pool balls around on the pool table and learn his colors and numbers. My mother, ever the teacher from the "old school", was mortified that he learned those from such a game. My dad, the pool player, was glad to know his grandson liked the game.

With other pre-school mothers, I formed a local TWIG branch, an auxiliary of Children's Hospital. We made crafts for an annual craft show with proceeds going to the hospital. Bill was very supportive making a cover for the pool table for our workspace. Over the years the table was lined with clothes pins painted as colonial soldiers, large and small stained blocks of wood as candle holders and large free standing wrapping paper organizers. The group made four or five items at our monthly meetings for a one day sale at the state fairgrounds with participating TWIG branches from Ohio. One year in charge of our craft table, I was terrified that our items would not sell and I would bring everything back to disappointed members. We did well that year selling some of the same handmade items as other branches.

Bill and I joined Welcome Wagon Bowling League. Bill had never bowled but was willing to learn, to get us out of the house together, and to meet Gahanna people. I had bowled in high school and with a teacher's league and loved the game. Monday nights we hired one of the neighbor girls to baby-sit and met many friends our age. We had fun teasing each other, challenging each other and sharing parenting stories. We bowled with the league three or four years and maintained our friendships. One couple I had known from college. The husband was the younger brother of "Wella" my college friend from Youngstown. He and his wife were then high school sweethearts when I visited Wella's family on long weekends away from Grove City College.

We played Euchre with friends from the bowling league and looked forward weekends to another "adult activity". When Barb and Bob came to our house for an evening game, Bob would walk into the house and ask, "Who wants to be rocked to sleep?" Behind his back he would be holding a large rock from my flower garden. The boys stood on the steps in their pajamas, waited for him to show the rock, then scrambled upstairs to bed. He became known as the boys' "Uncle Slug". We had good times and many laughs together. Bob brought out Bill's sense of humor. Bob worked for the railroad and always had a train story to tell.

When Lee started school, he rode a bus to kindergarten at a Gahanna church. That year the neighborhood school was too crowded for kindergarten. I would walk Lee to the bus stop and wait with him. Those dark mornings I wound glow-in-the-dark tape around his coat sleeves. I wanted him to be seen! From my experiences as a first grade teacher, I was afraid for my first born. I knew there could be bullies, teacher's pets, and loners. I prayed my first child could be happy out in the big world. It pained me to see my little boy board that big bus and be pulled away from me.

During the year, I became friends with the grandmotherly bus driver. She would later baby sit for our boys when I accompanied Bill on long business trips. Lee and I survived the year well. He had started reading by that time. For Mother's Day program he read "Caps for Sale" as the children acted out the story.

Our first years in Gahanna convinced us to stay in the Columbus area and raise our family, be known as the Hannas from Gahanna, and stay involved with the community and church.

One late November lunch time, I say, "I have a favor to ask of you."

"Oh?' Hilde says dropping her spoon in her cottage cheese.

"I need you to write some things in German."

"Why?"

I look up from my turkey sandwich. "Every Christmas one member of our family has to go on a scavenger hunt to find his/her present. Since Jay just came back from Germany, I'd like him to hunt for his gift."

"And you want me to write what?"

"Write the clues in German. I think it would surprise him and be fun for the family to follow him."

"How many will I write?"

"Next week I'll have four or five clues written for you to translate and give back before Christmas."

"Why not write them now?"

"I have to write them," I say. "And run through the course to make sure the clues are in order. It takes time."

"I'll try it, too." Hilde giggles as she returns to her lunch.

Chapter Seventeen

1966-1977
Columbus, Ohio

While Vietnam War continued, Nixon visited China and Saigon Airlift occurred, Bruni returned to Columbus, Ohio.

I arrived in Columbus, Ohio in January 1966. Again I stayed a few months with Ursula and her family, then rented a furnished apartment. I requested the Army to send my furniture which I had put in storage in Georgia. YJ refused to sign the papers so I never received my household goods. He sent me nasty letters with pictures of him with Vietnamese girls in provocative positions to make me jealous.

I got a job at Frito Lay working on the assembly line. It didn't pay much. David came to Ohio and begged me to come back to Georgia. I couldn't. I hated Georgia. It would have been senseless. David went to Vietnam soon after that. He wrote to me for several years. Because I could not make ends meet, paying rent and utilities, I worked second shift at Frito Lay. Susi started kindergarten. She didn't see much of me. My German friend, Giesela, took care of my girls while I worked. I had no car so I figured I would have to walk three miles to work and get home at midnight.

The first day I worked, I started walking home when a car stopped. A girl from work was driving with two other girls from work. Deana offered to pick me up from home daily and take me home like she did with the other girls. All of us lived in the same complex. Deana and I became the best of friends. That friendship would last for forty years. She also was divorced with three children at the time. Soon summer 1966 was almost over. Deana invited me to a concert. We went to see the Supremes, another time to see James Brown, Conway Twitty and Little Richard. Deana also drove the children and me to the beach at Buckeye Lake. She was good and kind to me.

A knock on the door came early on an August morning. I opened the door. There stood my husband. He came back from Vietnam, landed in San Francisco and bought a car. He drove to Ohio to see us. I had no idea he was coming. He had stayed the first night at Ursula's and Jim's because he went bar hopping with Jim. I don't know what else he did.

He said he did not want a divorce and was sorry about all the things that happened. He wanted to try one more time. I had actually enjoyed being alone, no other woman trouble. No lies. Life was nice and peaceful. Although I still loved him and wished he was different, I also knew that Susi loved her daddy. Peggy was afraid of him. I let him stay with me. He was to report to Ft. Bragg, North Carolina a month later. I took a few days off from work and we drove to Cosby, Tennessee to visit his parents. We stayed at a motel in Gatlinburg. I fell in love all over again, although we were legally separated. I got pregnant. I knew the next day. I was so upset and I cried and complained for weeks, until finally I had to accept it. When YJ first found out I was pregnant, he seemed to be happy, said he wanted a son and would move us to North Carolina.

We came back to Ohio and I went to work. One midnight YJ was supposed to pick me up. I told Deana not to wait for me. So I waited in the dark by the factory. No YJ. I ended up walking home. He came home around three a.m. from running around in bars. Later, I found a woman's wallet under the car seat. There were photos of a small blond and a driver's license. I confronted him and he said it was his friend's girlfriend's wallet. Before he left for North Carolina, he said he wanted to buy me a diamond wedding band and asked for my gold wedding band for size. I believed him. He left and I never saw him or the ring again. I never dreamed that I wouldn't hear from him. I was three months along when I saw him last.

After YJ went to North Carolina to report to the army, I didn't hear from him for weeks. I called and wrote numerous times but he would not come to the phone. I cried for months all through my pregnancy. I went to work daily, sick with morning sickness, and took care of my little Susi and Peggy when I came home at midnight from a long eight hours of work. It was hot and noisy in that potato chip factory. My girls were sleeping so peacefully when I came home. I laid down and cried for hours thinking about my situation, the silence from my husband and the uncertainty of what was to come.

I know I contemplated suicide. I wanted to die, but I wanted to take my girls with me. The possibility of my girls dying and for some reason I would still be alive, I changed my mind. I would not have been able to live without them or go to prison for murder. It was a terrible nightmare and I had no idea what was to come in all the months and years to come.

For many months I thought of YJ and the love I had for him. I missed him day and night. He called a few times and said he could not come for he had bad times with the car. One other call was to tell me that he was getting out of the army and coming to Columbus. He was going to find a job and live with us. In April he was discharged out of the army and disappeared. Patty was born the next month.

I waited one year for him. There was no more money from the army. Problems started all over again when I received a call from the loan company. They were looking for Mr. Gunter because he didn't make his car payments. I was not working. Patty was due and May 9, I went into the hospital. My dear friend Deana drove me, but could not stay with me. She had three children at home and was also working. My friend, Ursula, took care of my girls for three days.

I was devastated for I knew that my husband left me for another woman. Jim, Ursula's husband, called YJ's aunt's house in Tennessee and said he would call back that evening. He wanted YJ to be there. Jim told him "You have a healthy nine pound daughter. When are you coming to Ohio to assume your responsibilities?"

YJ said he was not coming "Just because." I received a letter from Aunt Mary that YJ was riding around the hills with a blond in the car. I was told his grandmother threw rocks at the car, she was so mad at him.

At the hospital I cried constantly and a nurse asked me why I was so upset. I finally confided in her and told her that my husband left and I had no money to pay rent and buy food. She contacted the Red Cross and a welfare department worker came to see me at the hospital. The caseworker asked if I had enough food for a week, if not someone would come to my house and talk to me.

Jim took me and Patty home. Some of the neighbors were wonderful. They brought me baby food, groceries and money. Deana brought me a chest full of baby clothing in various sizes up to two years. I had no money to buy baby things while waiting for my husband to provide for us.

A few weeks later I received a phone call from a woman looking for my husband. I told her he was not with me. She called several times and told me to go back to Germany where I belonged. One other woman called long distance. She was also with my husband and he left her, so she said. She offered to pay for our trips back to Germany. She mentioned that her parents were wealthy and she could pay for my trip. I could not figure out what that was all about.

The Welfare Department wanted me to stay home and take care of my little girls instead of working. I could not pay for a babysitter, rent and utilities and groceries from the small income. The state was going to find my husband. I waited for twenty years and nothing happened. Although I reported YJ's whereabouts several times, the state never attempted to collect child support. YJ always had a well paying job, yet he never sent any money.

When my baby Patty was a year old, I applied for a divorce. Susi was five, Peggy was four. Six months later the divorce became final. Soon I received a marriage announcement from Aunt Mary that YJ married that little blond. She was twenty and YJ twenty-eight. Not long after, they had two children.

When his mother scolded YJ about not sending me money for the support of his children, he told her that he loved his children and would send money. They received not one dime in thirty years! His mother was nice and his older sister Caroline was sweet, too. When Patty was a few weeks old, I received a package of baby things from them although they didn't have much money either.

I tried to make ends meet with the little money I got from Aid to Dependent Children. I babysat for four children. Soon I had as many as ten children in the apartment. I ironed baskets of laundry for people. I often stood in front of an ironing board until two a.m. After the children went to bed at promptly eight p.m., I started ironing. Little by little, I had enough money to buy a TV and used furniture so I would not have to pay so much rent for a furnished apartment. I moved to the first floor into an unfurnished place. It was easier for the children not to climb stairs.

In the building next to me lived a girl from England, her husband David and their two children. I loved Jean. She was funny and very outspoken. Whenever she was mad about something she said' "Bloody hell, there is something wrong with him or her." She came over quite often to visit.

One Christmas I managed to buy my children a doll and a toy and some clothes. Jean said "I have a lady friend who dresses like Santa Claus and comes to people's houses to visit the children." I was excited and asked her to see my little girls. I gave her the toys and she brought them in a sack. I had a very pretty Christmas tree in the corner and little Patty stood in her playpen holding onto the rails. My little Patty was walking when she was nine months old, she never crawled. Santa came with Jean and some other friends. My little Susi and Peggy and Patty were so excited. Their eyes got big. They talked to Santa clutching the new dolls in their arms. That was their first Christmas with a doll or a toy. The doll had a battery in the back. I turned it on and the doll laughed. My girls were so happy when they went to bed.

I had written a letter to David in Vietnam and told him that my husband left me and that I had a beautiful little girl named Patricia Ann. One day I received a large package from him with wonderful Vietnamese things. He also told me that he got married before he went to Vietnam. He needed someone to come home to. It was alright with me. He deserved someone who loved him.

In the summer of 1968 a young couple moved in upstairs. They had a new baby and the young man's name was Chuck. He was about twenty-six. He always hung around one little girl outside in the parking lot. The little girl, Angela, went for rides with him. She lived next door and often played alone outside days when her parents were sleeping. Jean came over to my place at noon. As she looked through my living room window, she noticed Chuck lifting Angela down from the hood of his car with his hands under her dress. Jean said, "Bloody hell, there is something wrong with this guy. Did you see his hands under her dress?" Angela was crying.

I turned to my little Susi and asked if Chuck ever touched her. She said that he didn't do anything to her. A few days later, he knocked on my door and asked if he could put a little bicycle together for my Susi. She was excited to get a little bike, and I told him that would be great. A week went by and word got around that Chuck and his young wife moved during the night. Susi was listening. Again I asked if he did anything to her. She was quiet for a minute and then asked if he really moved. I said yes that he was not coming back. Susi then told me he took her pants down in the storage and played with her. "He said I would not get a bike if I didn't let him do that. I wanted the bike." Peggy was listening and added that he did it to her also.

Jean and I were speechless. In 1968 no one talked about those things. I called the police. A detective came and took a statement. He went to Angela's house and her fat mother refused to give a report saying she didn't want her little girl in court. I told the detective that Chuck would take Angela for a ride and she'd be screaming when they came back holding an ice cream cone in her little hand. The detective told Angela's mother that by refusing to file a report, Chuck would someday kill a little girl, raping her first. That did not faze her. She wanted nothing to do with this crime. She need not worry for children under the age of eighteen did not have to testify nor would their names be in the paper.

I lived with my three little girls in Beverlee Manor. There were about six to eight hundred apartments. They were pretty nice then, six tenants in each building. We lived there seven years. My girlfriend Deanna and I were going out sometimes on weekends. After I took care of eight to ten children six days a week and with all the ironing I did, I needed to get out sometimes. I loved to dance.

I met a nice guy named Lee and we dated for two years. Nothing came of this relationship for he told me he didn't want to take care of three children. I was also told that from another guy named Ron.

One Saturday Deanna and I went out to a dance hall. The band was great and the bandleader came and sat at our table during breaks. As we were sitting there, I noticed a guy looking at me quite often. He was sitting at the bar. He was cute, but short. After a while he asked me to dance and he was a wonderful dancer and so polite, soft spoken and a gentleman. His name is Bernard, Bernie for short. He asked me if he could see me sometime. He told me he was stationed at Rickenbacher Air Base in the air force as a sergeant. I saw him again at the Brass Rail a week later, and we danced and talked.

One day he called and asked if I wanted to go for a ride with the children. The girls were excited for they liked to ride in a car. He took us to MacDonalds. The girls loved that for I never went there with them. They liked French fries like all children do. Bernard and I started dating. He didn't seem to mind my girls, but I could tell that he was controlling. I tried to put it out of my mind.

He invited me to go to Waco, Texas with him to meet his parents, so we drove there. My neighbor took care of the girls. Patty was sweet, two-years-old and potty- trained. Bernie paid the babysitter. At first, his family was nice. He has four sisters and four brothers. I did not care for his parents too much. The mother was manipulating and his old father had a roaming eye. That should have told me something, for Bernie was a lot like his father.

He got discharged from the air force after nine years and got a good job at Western Electric in Columbus. He stayed in the Air Force Reserve. When Patty was three-years-old, Bernie proposed to me and decided to buy a house. I was happy for I wanted my children to have a father, and I wanted a house. I never had one before.

We got married at a preacher's house. It was the third marriage for me and second for Bernie. The father-in-law of Anita, another German girlfriend, was the preacher. Anita and her husband were our witnesses. We had cake and the preacher's wife played the piano. The children were not included in the ceremony because we drove ninety miles to another town and later we went to a restaurant for dinner.

A few months later we went on our honeymoon to Texas if you can call it a honeymoon. We drove without the children to Texas by car. Bernie said we couldn't take the children for we were driving all the way to California and Mexico. The girls stayed at our house with an old, dear lady friend. She needed the money, and she loved my girls.

On our trip Bernie never gave me a quarter to buy a Pepsi. When we stopped at a gas station to go to the bathroom or to get gas, I had to ask my brother-in-law for money. When we started out in Texas to drive to California, my brother-in-law, Edward and his girlfriend and my father-in-law, Tony went along. I hated sitting in the front of the car in the middle between Bernie and Tony. He put his hand on my thigh and Bernie told him to stop. The air-conditioner in the car quit in Nevada. It was extremely hot. Edward and Maryanne were lying in the back seat. I wanted desperately to lie down for awhile. We did not stay at a motel overnight. They took turns driving. After a few days we arrived at his sister Helen's house in Los Angeles.

Helen, the oldest sister, was married with six children. She was nice. Bernie started to really boss me around or ignore me completely. He wanted to impress the family by showing them that he was the boss. A few days later, we were driving to Disneyland. It was lunch time and nobody was ready yet, except Bernie and me. I told him and the rest of the family to get a move on. That made him angry and I couldn't believe what happened. He kicked me in the rear in front of everybody. Helen got angry with Bernie and Edward told him "Shame on you." My father-in-law, Tony said, "If you don't like the way Bernie treats you, be quiet or get out". I realized then that I had made a mistake again by marrying another abusive man.

The trip was not enjoyable anymore. On the way to Mexico again I had no money. Bernie decided what to buy and when to eat. We went sightseeing in Universal Studios, and we went to Las Vegas on the way back. Tony stayed in Los Angeles-no more pawing my thigh. In Las Vegas we did not see shows. Bernie wanted to go to go-go bars. Maryanne played the slot machines. I had no money to play anything. Finally we drove back to Ohio. I was disillusioned about the trip and glad to see my girls.

Back in Columbus we loved our house. The girls had their own rooms and a large yard. It was a ranch style brick home with air conditioning, new appliances and a washer and dryer. I should have been happy, and I was for awhile until I had no money of my own. Bernie kept the checkbook and took the check I received from Welfare for my girls.

Bernie started to buy a mobile home and a boat. He owned two cars and his whole paycheck was tied up in loans. Soon he resented me not working and not contributing to the household. Anita cleaned houses and asked me to work with her. When I brought home a check, Bernie took it.

Bernie would pinch Patty's cheeks very hard when she was bad or when she cried. She screamed when he pinched her. He also twisted her ears. I had fights with him. Susi became quiet. She was now ten or eleven. I noticed that she didn't like Bernie.

When I decided to marry him, I had a talk with Susi and asked her how she felt about my getting married. She was excited and wanted me to have a husband and her, a father. I also told my girls to report to me if their stepfather ever touched them in the wrong places. They promised they would. Susi then told me that she hated having to kiss her stepfather on the lips when she went to bed. Susi still loved and missed her father.

I became homesick for Germany. My daughter Petra was fourteen-years-old and wanted to see me. She missed her mother, I know. Grandmother Maria and Heinrich, Petra's *Vater*, did not dare let Petra come to America for fear of my kidnapping her. Bernie finally let me go and paid four hundred dollars for the round trip ticket and gave me five hundred dollars for spending money. That did not go far. Of course, he had to go somewhere, too. He planned to go with his friends in a mobile home to Texas, California and Mexico, so he needed money. His mother came from Texas to cook for the girls for a few weeks and returned to Texas in the mobile home with Bernie.

It would have cost too much for the girls to go to Germany with me. My family and my *Vater* had never met my children. I decided to visit my *Vater* because of his age. We had been estranged for thirteen years. I had never been on a plane and was afraid to fly. I had come to America by ship ten years earlier.

I arrived in Germany at my sister's house thirty-six hours later. Everyone was happy to see me. My *Vater* cried crocodile tears when he saw me. I stayed at my ex-mother-in-law's house for two weeks. Petra's *Vater* came daily to his mother's house to bother me. Heinz followed Petra and me. Drunk, he harassed me daily. It was embarrassing. His wife lived up on the hill. She cried daily for he told her their marriage was not valid, only the marriage with me was recognized in God's eyes. He told her he still loved me.

I told Maria I was going to stay with my sister. Petra was spending a lot of time with her boyfriend Jürgen, who became her husband when she turned eighteen. Her father-in-law didn't approve of the marriage for he knew that Petra's *Vater* was a drunkard and made his wives work. My visit to Germany was very nice but after four weeks, I was glad to come home to my husband and children.

We were married three years when Bernie told me he had a sexual disease, gonorrhea. He told me to go to the doctor. I fell out of the sky. All this time I was thinking that all was well in the bedroom and that we had a healthy sex life. With all the sex we had together, he still was not satisfied. I was stunned and very unhappy. It was like I was dreaming. I saw our doctor and after examination, it turned out I was fine. It had been several weeks that Bernie did not approach me for sex, and I was puzzled. He was going somewhere else.

I received phone calls from friends who also worked at Western Electric and was told that my husband was seeing women in other departments and asking them out on dates. Money was tight, and I realized I needed to find a job. I started working at a plastic factory and worked sixty hours a week.

I worked the day shift and Bernie worked second. We didn't see much of each other except in bed at night. I was contemplating what to do. I knew my marriage was over, I could not trust him any longer, but I didn't want a divorce then for I loved Bernie. I didn't want to give up my home. I loved the house. It was beautiful and we kept it clean. Bernie was a fanatic when it came to cleanliness.

One Saturday, I came home early. Susi was crying. She was fifteen. She had a very developed body and long blond hair. She told me that Bernie came into her room without knocking. He was clever in keeping the vacuum cleaner in Susi's closet, a reason to go in there. She was undressed from the waist up, and she was very embarrassed. I confronted Bernie and I told Susi to lock her door anytime she wanted privacy. In time, Bernie forbade her to lock her door. He would punish her. One day he went into Peggy's room and jerked the covers off her as she was sleeping. She was nude from the waist up. She was so startled and grabbed the covers. She was fourteen.

Bernie was getting worse. When we wanted to watch a program on TV, he kept switching the channels. The girls gave up and went to bed with Susi hating to kiss him. I did not know any longer what to do. We argued about my paycheck every payday because I wanted to keep some money, but he insisted he get the paycheck.

I decided to take the overtime pay and apply for my own savings account. He went berserk. "I'll get a divorce if you withhold money". He still received my regular forty hour a week pay, but that was not enough. I had the savings account in my name. He had our savings account in his name at the credit union at Western Electric. I did not know how much money he had. I had about six-hundred and fifty dollars in the savings.

One day I looked in the book and all but fifty dollars was gone. The bank paid him even though the account was in my name only. Later when I applied for a divorce, on my lawyer's advice, I went to the bank. They could not understand why they paid him and agreed to pay me back.

At that time, Bernie was unemployed and I felt sorry for him. I dropped the matter and let him have the money. My attorney was furious.

When I was still cleaning houses, Bernie took me to one house where I cleaned every other week. I had no driver's license. He dropped me off and picked me up. The lady was nice and old and very ill. Bernie met the husband and wife. One morning when I got there the lady went back to bed for she felt ill. Her husband went to the library and should have been home soon. I proceeded to clean out the refrigerator. The door opened in the kitchen, and the mister entered. When he saw me with my back turned to him, he approached from behind and put his hands on my breasts. I told him "You remove your hands right this minute or else".

He ignored me and whispered, "Ah come on, let's go to the couch. I pay you twenty-five dollars if you let me do it to you." I was mad. His wife was in the bedroom and this man suggested such a thing. I finished my work and went home with Bernie. I did not say a word to Bernie. Two weeks later he woke up in the morning and asked why I didn't go to this couple's house that day. I finally told him. He was surprised and proceeded to say "Oh come on now, that nice old man wouldn't do a thing like that. I met him. He is nice. You just don't want to go to work because you are lazy." I told him then and there that I would divorce him. I was sick of him always taking other people's side.

There were instances at work. A black man grabbed me between my legs. I had witnesses saying I minded my business while I was working on my machine. The man got a slap on the wrist at the office when I reported the incident. My husband said I was leading the guy on, he would not do a thing like that.

One other time, my husband said we would visit a lady and her husband at their house. Rose was from his hometown. He was excited to know her. Susi went with us. They had a daughter about sixteen. She had been in a lot of trouble already with drugs, but she was a beauty with long black hair and beautiful build. She invited Susi to her room. We talked in the living room. Ralph, the husband, had nothing to say. Rose was the boss.

I could tell she had a thing for my husband. Bernie, at that time, looked very handsome with beautiful black hair and dark eyes. Often the women would stop the car at the house to talk to him when he was working in the yard. They would comment on the lawn. I thought it was funny. I trusted my husband. I told Bernie on the way home that Rose had the "hots" for him. He told me I was crazy.

A few months later we separated. I'd had enough. He lived in his camper. It was winter. I felt sorry for him. We went back together. Susi was upset that he came back. I had no idea that in the meantime he was going to Rose's house to eat when her husband was not home. It was mind-boggling. He had an eye on Rose's daughter and at the same time was having sex with Rose.

One Sunday the phone rang. Rose asked to talk to Bernie. I laughed and said, "Your girlfriend is on the phone." I handed him the phone. I heard him say, "I came back to my wife because I wanted to. Yes, I care for her and the kids." Rose was furious because she lost him. Several weeks later I came home from work, and Bernie was home on vacation. Susi was crying loudly, sobbing. I asked what is wrong.

Susi told me that Rose came to the high school with the daughter and knocked her against the locker and punched her. She accused Susi of stealing a ring out of Cheryl's room. Susi assured me that she didn't take the ring. We had visited months ago. Bernie ordered me to change clothes. We were going to Rose's house.

I told him to call Rose and tell her to come to our house and bring a policeman. The daughter had once attacked her mother with a butcher knife. No way was I setting foot in that house again.

Rose never showed. I knew about this whole picture. Rose was mad because she couldn't have Bernie and figured she could get him back by causing trouble between us. The principal at the high school threw Rose and Cheryl out. Bernie picked Susi up and threatened to beat her if she didn't produce the ring. I knew Susi didn't take the ring for on that visit she had no pockets in her pantsuit and no pocket book.

Months later Rose called again to invite us to her son's graduation. Bernie wanted to go. I had a fit. He told Rose on the phone in my presence that he didn't believe Susi took the ring and for her not to ever call again. But the damage was done.

Again I separated from Bernie and finally got the divorce. A legal separation did not work for he was not willing to divide properties. He wanted to keep the house, the mobile home, the boat and the cars, except my car. I taught myself to drive and got my license and a car which was to be a birthday present from him. At the divorce I was told to pay for it. The judge ordered the house sold and the profit divided between us. Bernie was furious for he had to move out. He assaulted me and slapped me so hard I fell.

The house was sold one month later, Bernie moved to a beautiful new home, and I moved with my girls to Whitehall, a suburb of Columbus.

Hilde, in hot pants, and her Vater reconciled
on this trip to Germany 1973.

Chapter Eighteen

1970-1987
Seattle, Washington and Gahanna, Ohio

While the Watergate Scandal broke, two gasoline crises occurred, and Mt Saint Helen's erupted, Peg's family grew.

One of Bill's early assignments, a research project at Washington University Hospitals, took us to Seattle Washington. We spent the summer of 1971 on the Battelle campus near the university where his project consisted of making a mathematical model of the left side of the heart. These were the first days of heart catherization and models were used for doctors' visualization for the process. Bill and a colleague from University Hospitals worked together to map the heart for doctors to test there and in Columbus.

Greg was nine months and Lee three-years-old. Battelle rented us a two-bedroom bungalow and provided a crib and diaper service for three months. Our little house sat at the fringe of Battelle's beautifully landscaped campus of modern buildings, offices, meeting rooms and housing. Bill could walk across our backyard to his office.

Fully equipped and furnished hotel rooms and apartments sat on the grounds for visitors staying shorter terms. The campus was a fascinating place with visiting researchers from all over the world. We felt privileged to be there!

In this world of academia and sophistication, we were quickly reminded that we were parents first. In our first hours there we had to call Poison Control. Greg had toddled into the house, headed for the first floor bathroom and eaten a bar of soap! We were told he'd be OK, but to call him "Bubbles" for a few days.

Wednesday afternoons, I attended a social hour, met other men and their wives assigned there, and made friends from all over the world. One woman, an American, married to an Indian demographer, introduced me to this academic/social/ intellectual world. I felt the eyes of others watching this young wife in a new social situation. Like the army officer's wife, I was again following established rules.

Sometimes I took a break, hired a babysitter and explored Seattle on my own. I would hear one of my mother's mom-isms. "Take a day for yourself."

We enrolled Lee in a preschool playgroup at a nearby church. I would drive him there, drive back and settle Greg into an afternoon nap. Ours were the youngest children in the Battelle community. Lee needed to be with others his age. It rained daily, but mornings I pulled the boys in a wagon in the drizzle through the surrounding area of stately homes and manicured lawns and dreamed of where we might live someday.

Other days the boys and I enjoyed library story hours and borrowing books. Evenings when Bill came home and the rains stopped, we would eat dinner and drive to the beach. Descending the hills to the beach we would sing a song of "Around and Round and Down". The boys and I would play among the stacked rocks and warm sand, and watch red and purple streaked sunsets over the water while Bill took photos of trains traveling between the beach and the surrounding hills. Seattle with its majestic Mount Rainier rising above the clouds, noisy waterfront fish markets and lush green residential areas gave us a different view of our country from the flat farm lands of Ohio.

Bill's colleague at the University of Washington, his wife and their two pre-teens became good friends. They introduced us to Seattle with drives in the snow to Mt. Rainier, hikes and picnics at Lake Louise and relaxing weekends at their summer home on Miller River. We were pleasantly surprised to feel a connection with their family when we discovered that the wife's father had helped build the railroad for the steel mill in our hometown in Pennsylvania!

One weekend at Miller River, we were sleeping in the guest cabin next to the railroad tracks. We knew trains passed nearby, but didn't know the schedule, nor had we realized how close the cabin sat to the tracks. After we had gone to bed for the night, a train approached in the darkness and startled us with its bright light and roaring rumble. The cabin shook. The room lit up. The boys screamed. Shaken, Bill and I each grabbed one son. "It scared me, too. It's only a train." We said, "It's gone now." Then we laughed, reminded of our fright the first night in our first apartment when a tugboat and its search light had scared the two of us.

Greg celebrated his first and second birthdays in Seattle. We spent a second summer there in 1972 for the completion of Bill's project. We enjoyed meals of "melt in your mouth salmon", toured the battleship at Bellingham, and viewed the magnificent Snoqualime Falls.

That second summer, Battelle rented us a three-bedroom house away from campus. The Jewish owners had gone to Israel for three months. I told all "The kitchen may have held kosher food when we entered, but not for long." I knew kosher kitchens had separate dishes for dairy and meat. Not knowing which, I used all the dishes. The front windows had a great view of snow-capped Mt. Rainier. We could watch the mountain "come out" of the clouds.

Near the end of the stay, we returned to Pennsylvania for my dad's needed heart surgery. Afraid I would lose him, I wanted to see him again and support my mother. Bill flew to Pittsburgh with me and the boys, and returned to Seattle to complete his assignment. His parents met us in Pittsburgh and took the boys to Edinboro Lake to stay with them where they were vacationing. I went immediately with my mother to see my dad. I had been strong for as long as I could. Strain and emotion overwhelmed me, and I passed out in the hallway. I became no support for my mother.

***

Bill and I returned to our home on Heil Drive where we raised our six children.

Jay Robert was born in January 1975. Lee was in school all day and Greg in preschool. Greg had just turned five in August. I knew from teaching first grade, the differences in boys and girls development to wait another year for his starting kindergarten. I took a lot of "flak" from friends and neighbors for the delay, but I knew I was doing the right thing for him. Greg did well in school because of the decision.

Bill's parents came the week Jay was born. We played Euchre the night before his birth, knowing that I would go to the hospital to be induced the next morning. Jay Robert is named for the blue jays in our back yard and for our fun-loving friend Bob. When another healthy Hanna boy and I came home, we were isolated in the bedroom. The two older boys had chicken pox. I only saw Bill and his mom behind masks. We were extremely careful and frightened as the virus can be fatal to an infant. Jay and I spent a week getting acquainted while Bill and his parents took care of Lee and Greg.

That spring we went to Florida to visit my parents. Photos show my parents holding baby Jay while Bill and I are in the pool with Lee and Greg wearing "swimmies", air filled arm bands. We took the "Auto Train" to have our own car in Florida. We took the boys to Disneyworld and stayed in a nearby motel. My mother stayed there with the baby and I went into the park with Bill and my Dad until it was time to nurse Jay. I would exit the grounds with a pass, walk to the motel, feed Jay and re-enter to meet the family. I wanted to experience Disneyworld and see it through my children's eyes. It was an exhausting week. For many of the following years we visited my parents in Florida during their three-month stays and the children's spring breaks.

When Jay was a year old, Bill's father died. He and Mom had spent Christmas with us and we all enjoyed the boys and their activities. They returned to their retirement home Dad built at Edinboro Lake. A few weeks later, early one morning, Mom phoned. "Dad suffered a massive heart attack last night. He died at midnight. Please call Bill at work." I shook as I made the call. Dad was the first of our parents to die. We knew the day would come, and as only children we were close to our parents. I sat for a minute and said a prayer that I could tell Bill without crying and be a strong support for him. We all went back for the funeral and to help Mom, then she was left alone in the beautiful new home overlooking the lake.

In March of 1976 Bill and I went on a Marriage Encounter weekend which renewed our marriage, our love for each other and our faith. Our friends from Akron had been on a weekend and recommended we attend one in Columbus. Bill mentioned this at work and a couple we knew had been on a weekend and volunteered to baby-sit for the three boys. We took them up on it for a weekend away! We were asked to become active in the movement and another couple volunteered to baby-sit while we went to Chicago to train as presenters.

For six years we shared our marriage and experiences on weekend retreats for couples who wanted to strengthen their marriages. Later, we went to Chicago and trained to start Engaged Encounter weekends in Columbus for engaged couples and shared our experiences of love and faith for another six years. We were also involved in presenting parish and diocesan Pre-Cana sessions. We believe in communication in relationships, the basis for all three movements.

Our children stayed with other families during the weekends we presented. They learned that we weren't the only parents who required them to wash hands before meals, try new foods and say prayers at bedtimes. They learned to get along with children of all ages. As we dropped our children off at one household, the mother reassured me. "Don't forget you are leaving them with another mother."

Years later while presenting our first Engaged Encounter weekend in Columbus, tornado warnings sounded. We had to usher the couples to the basement of the old school where the weekend was presented. Nine months pregnant with Kristin, I was watched closely by the engaged couples constantly asking, "Are you OK? How do you feel? Would you please sit down?" I reassured the team and the couples that I was always induced and would not deliver that weekend.

We retired from presenting weekends when it became too difficult to manage our children's activities, Bill's travel schedules and updating and reading our "talks".

***

One Thanksgiving Bill's mom came to spend the holiday with us. She wasn't feeling well. When she returned home, she was diagnosed with pancreatic cancer. Bill went back to Edinboro to spend the week after Christmas with her. She died six weeks later. We went back for the funeral and took the boys. Jay was three and I questioned taking him to see her. We were advised to take him to the funeral home for closure, but not to the funeral. Jay couldn't stop asking "Why is Grandma sleeping in the pretty baby bed?" Lee, ten and Greg, eight and I had a discussion about death. They asked if I would die some day and I answered "Yes." They cried, then asked, "Who will bake us brownies?" Then I hugged them and we all cried thinking of our being apart.

In August 1979, we had just found out I was pregnant with Stephen, and had come back from the bittersweet sale of the Hanna family farm north of Columbus, the end of the Hanna farming family in Ohio. We drove back into Gahanna into torrential rains and flooding on Heil Drive.

The flood of the century, result of Hurricane Fredrick, brought high water throughout our neighborhood. Men paddled down our street in canoes. Sump pumps overflowed and basement walls collapsed. Bill went out to help others. Our house was safe, but I wasn't. I started bleeding heavily. Fearing I would lose the baby, I called neighbors who were a doctor and a nurse for help. They came, had me lie down and raise my feet and called my doctor. He told them to get me to the hospital immediately.

There was no way to get there. Cars could not get through the high water. Another neighbor offered his "off road" pick up. I would not chance that ride! When I did get to the doctor's a few days later, I was ordered off my feet for six weeks. We had help with meals, babysitting and encouragement from friends. At times, it was hard to ask for help as Bill and I are only children and used to being independent.

That September my birthday present was a new sliding glass door, so I could look at the world clearly as I lay on the couch in the family room. After the first three months of rest and reading all the books on my list, I was able to function normally. With three boys and another on the way, my days were hectic resuming childcare, housework and carpooling.

We needed more room and in October started adding a master suite over the attached garage. I watched the shell go up and heard the workmen everyday add something new. That spring, I wanted to stand inside and see the rooms and their views. Very pregnant with Stephen, I was passed through an inside window opening on my back by our friend Dave and Bill. I looked like a whale floating in air!

Stephen Richard was born in March 1980. Induced, he was healthy after our rough start. With Jay in preschool, all the boys were in school. We quickly got used to having a baby in the house again.

Many late nights we sat baby Stephen in a swing in the unfinished rooms of the addition while Bill and I dry-walled. Bill taught the older boys to hang dry wall, install plumbing and electrical wiring. When he was growing up, Bill helped his dad refinish a room each year and wanted that experience for our boys. During the plumbing phase he stationed each boy with a bucket under a joint in a major pipe. "What do we do?" the boys asked. Bill turned the water on and said, "Yell if you get wet!" We enjoyed our new bedroom, office and bathroom for many years. With each additional child, the office became a nursery and back again to an office.

Kristin Marie was born in April 1982, the first girl in the Hanna family in seventy-five years! After an easy pregnancy, she was induced as were her brothers. Friends decorated the trees in the front yard with pink ribbons and pasted a sign on the garage door. IT'S A GIRL! More little girl clothes than she could ever wear came from family and friends. When she was announced at the boys' school, they couldn't believe it, nor could their parents who called Bill to verify that the Hannas had a girl.

When Kristin was a month old, we drove our family back to visit my folks. We arrived late at night. Mother was in bed. I woke her to introduce her to her only granddaughter. Mother sat up in bed and I laid Kristin next to her. Smiling, Mother said, "Now you have someone to take care of you." I thought that was a strange statement to make as I had Bill and the boys. I count all my family as mainstays.

When Kristin was only a few months old, we took the family cross country by train. The trip had been planned the year before we knew about her. Each of the three big boys had his suitcase and a baby item to carry. Bill carried two-year-old Stephen in a back pack. I carried Kristin in a front pack. One of the boys carried Stephen's diaper bag, another Kristin's diaper bag and another the collapsible bed filled with disposable diapers. A photo of us at six in the morning at a Seattle train station shows us ready to board the train carrying our "baggage". Each carries his two pieces of luggage.

Traveling on the train was a great experience for all. There was always somebody on board for the boys to play cards with, a grandmother who wanted to hold the baby while we ate and only two hours of entertaining two-year-old Stephen for each of the older boys. The rocking motion of the train lulled everyone to sleep. I nursed Kristin which made it easy to travel with an infant. At times when I close my eyes, I can still see the white moon reflected off Coeur du Lac, Idaho as I nursed her early one morning. The train traveled on a low bridge and it seemed as if we were gliding across the lake! I experienced the simple beauty of nourishing my child in the simple beauty of moonlight on water.

Bill and the boys followed the train's route on a map. As we traveled through the Cascade Mountains, they saw the sunshine off the shed Bill had helped build at the campsite at Miller River when we had been there in "70's.

***

Roy Austin was born in January 1984, another easy pregnancy. He was named by his brothers for their grandfathers. Bill was with me at the last three births. He was not allowed in the delivery room when the first three were born. At the last delivery, I was induced in early morning as usual. The doctor said if the baby was not born before noon, I would be sent home. I told him "Not to worry, I would deliver before lunch". Roy was born at 11:30. All the nurses were coming to see the white-haired lady who was still having babies!

Our mothers came when the first three were born and each stayed a week to help with cooking, cleaning and childcare. When the last three were born, my friends came as Bill's mother had died and my mother could no longer travel. My childhood friends, Joyce from Maryland came when Stephen was born, Carolee came from Pennsylvania when Kristin was born and brought three years of little girls clothes from her daughter. Our friend Alice, from Akron, Ohio came when Roy was born. Without biological sisters, I am blessed with good friends who have become soul sisters.

With sixteen years between Roy and Lee, I wondered if the two would know each other. I saw the bond between them when we went to see Lee at college on Parents Day. I dressed eight-month-old Roy in "cords" and a sweater. He looked like a miniature Joe College. Lee was very proud to show him around the dorm. They've become caring brothers. In this spread of sixteen years I was washing diapers, ironing three white shirts a day for Bill, Lee and Greg for prep school, feeding teenage boys, caring for toddlers and nursing a baby. In spite of it all I tried not to complain. Motherhood was my job! I nursed all six babies. It was the one time in my days I could sit down without feeling guilty!

***

November 1984 Ronald Reagan was re-elected President of the United States and Jay was hospitalized. At dinnertime, I found him under the basement steps sobbing. "I'm so lonely,' he said "The big boys have each other and you are busy with the little ones." He continued. "I am the only one with brown hair and brown eyes, the only left-hander." Everything he said was true. I was shaken to the core of my motherhood. I called Bill downstairs. We let Jay talk, horrified to hear how sad he was. I slept with him that night afraid of what he might do.

We kept him home from school the next day, and I made phone calls for help. Bill, Jay and I met with a psychologist and Jay was admitted to OSU Hospital. We were terrified. We were entrusting our son's care to strangers. We told Jay "We can't help you. We have to take you to people who can." Jay was willing to go. He was nine. At the hospital, Bill and I fell sobbing into each others arms. We called for our friend, Fr. Pete who was in the area. The three of us prayed for healing and strength. We knew a crisis could make or break a marriage.

Jay received medication for a chemical imbalance and sensory integration therapy, stayed caught up on school work, got needed glasses and returned home a happier boy. He started back to school with a different teacher who understood his situation. There he met a life-long friend Patrick. Jay thrived in this class and stayed active in scouting and developed a circle of loyal friends.

It was hard to explain to friends and family that a nine-year-old suffered from depression. My parents understood only when I told them Jay had a nervous breakdown. We had moral support and prayers from friends, yet I would lean on the washer and cry for the sadness in my child.

***

All our children walked to the nearby elementary school, rode their bikes to the swimming pool and walked over the hill to the supermarket. They had neighborhood playmates near their ages. Bill and I became involved in their schools. For twenty years, I volunteered to read my children's favorite books once a month in each child's classroom. A younger brother or sister sat in a stroller at my side.

One winter during the "Energy Crisis", the children were home from school. One school opened one day a week for class and one week's assignments were sent home. Parents were to instruct their children and keep them up to date for the next week's class. The boys and I had school at home everyday. My training as a teacher kept us organized and on task.

Bill traveled all over the world for his job, many were long trips. I didn't mind "running the show" during the week. When he stayed weekends, I needed help. Our house was on a well-traveled street and many friends stopped for tea during the day. They knew I'd be home and seeking adult company. I enjoyed their stays and they said they enjoyed seeing little kids again.

A friend and I were having tea one day and looked up to see three-year-old Kristin standing in the doorway with her face totally covered in lipstick. My friend dropped her teacup and screamed. Stephen came up behind his sister and said, "Look Mommy, she's an Indian." I calmly told him where to find the cold cream to clean her face! My friend was speechless.

I don't remember being as tired as I was in those days. It was all I could do to get meals, clean the kitchen and keep up with the laundry. An avid reader, I could only read Reader's Digest condensed novels. Music became my helper. When I felt overwhelmed, I sat in a rocker away from the children and listened to the soothing music from the movie "Out of Africa". At these times I remembered my mother playing the piano when she was upset. Prayers for strength also helped. When people asked how I did it all, I would say, "I say my prayers, and keep moving or I fall asleep."

In those same years, I became friends with Alice who lived across the street. She was single mom raising a son with Cerebral Palsy. Her mother lived with her and Bernice became our morning "Wake Up Call" She would call our house at six-thirty a.m. and if she didn't see lights on at our house, she would call again. Bill and I were so tired those days that we didn't hear our alarm clocks. We missed Bernice's calls when she passed.

After work and when Alice retired on disability, we discussed the problems of the world many evenings. We could talk about anything and read many of the same books. Later when she was bedridden with emphysema, I would go to her home one day a week and read to her. One evening her son called "She's failing," he said. "You should come." I rushed to say good-bye to a dear friend and confidant. Alice and I had a strong friendship and admitted we were "daddy's girls". In remembrance, I wrote a poem entitled "Alice's Legacy" ending with the lines

> "Voice whispering
> Heart failing
> She breathed her last
> And left us
> To listen"

My strengths came from Bill's and my love, friends, prayers and yearly trips with Bill. Each winter we attended the annual conference of a professional engineering society of which he was a member. We hired someone to stay with the kids for a long weekend away. The trips were my energy shot in the arm for the year. Bill and I visited many major cities in our country and the world. I toured with the wives while Bill attended or presented sessions. When I could attend one of his presentations, I sat proudly seeing my husband's business side.

On one trip, we flew into Paris and missed our connecting flight to Geneva, Switzerland. My ability to speak French came back as I had to get us on another flight. After Bill's meetings in Geneva, we took the train through the Black Forest and into Frankfort, Germany where he'd scheduled meetings. Bill's knowledge of German helped us get the correct trains at the correct times. On one train we met the "Ugly American", the bumbling traveler in garish clothes, who bragged loudly. We were embarrassed for the impression he gave of our countrymen and hid our faces in our books!

Years later we traveled to England with a British colleague who took us by train to his family home. We had proper afternoon tea with his mother. Being in England was at times overwhelming standing in places older than our country. We went onto Bath for a conference where I spent days shopping with a British wife of another presenter. One evening we had a formal dinner with the Lord Mayor and dinner another evening in the Pump House of the Roman baths. We were entranced to be amid ancient history. Bill and I traveled to Chester to visit another colleague who had been to the states. A pleasant host, he and his wife took us to a local pub, hosted dinner in their home and a boat ride on a nearby lake. At one point, we stood on a wall in Chester made by the Romans and looked into Wales. We wished we'd had time to visit there.

***

Back on Heil Drive, Bea was one of my "stop-in friends". Two of our older children were the same ages. As "Patience personified", she taught me that there could be grey sides to situations. I saw things as black or white, right or wrong. We had many discussions as she dealt with my bluntness. Bea bought me a tape of Billy Joel's song "Honesty" saying that was me. On one visit, she sat with me on the couch and held my hand as she told me, "We're moving to Memphis. Dave has accepted a job there." I felt the white hot knife slice through me again, jolting me into realization that life changes and I can't stop it.

Bill and I hired household help after a day of sheer terror. I looked out the window and recognized two little red coats standing on another major road. Stephen and Kristin! I tore out of the house, screaming and running along our street. I ran in and out of neighbors' fenced in backyards. I couldn't get to my children! The police had been called and a patrolman took my children to the side of the road as I screamed "I'm coming! I'm coming." Then I remembered that I had left my baby in the crib in an unlocked house! I collapsed in the grass and asked the policeman to stay with us while I caught my breath. Back at home, I called Bill and told him I needed help again. That summer, Emily, a teenage daughter of our friends, became my "mother's helper".

We had several housekeepers over the years. Fran came to clean house that fall. For one day a week in the five years that followed, she brought her disabled son who lay on the couch and enjoyed watching our household activities. Our children entertained him and learned to accept people as people with differences.

With five boys and a girl, our family had our share of childhood diseases and allergies, stitches and broken bones, lost children and hospital visits. Bill and I managed to survive with help of prayers, friends and our close knit family. We had no relatives in the area. We needed to create our own family and our older boys learned to help take care of the younger children. When the older boys were left to babysit the younger ones, Lee didn't stand for foolishness. Greg played with them and read to them in funny voices. Jay was the middle child who was too young to babysit and too old to be constantly watched.

It was not unusual to have one more additional children join us for dinner. I always said, "What I cooked for a meal would have been a small dinner party for my mother." There were sleepovers on the weekends with Lee's friends. Greg's friends came the next weekend. Bill said, "Over the years only the faces changed". The boys would plan their moves for strategy games and all meet the next weekend playing on the pool table cover in the basement. Jay had sleepovers where the boys brought flashlights and played cards inside an in-door tent. Kristin had slumber parties as well. I would plan in-house or neighborhood scavenger hunts for the girls. Most of Roy's "overnights" were with Boy Scouts. Jay, Kristin and Roy were active in scouting and Bill and I were involved in their activities.

***

In 1987 my mother died after years of deteriorating health. In the months before she died, it became impossible for my dad to take care of her. I went back to Aliquippa and visited nursing homes with him. Our first choice wasn't right for Mother. Her health continued to fail and she entered the hospital. She recovered and we chose a larger nursing home. She didn't want to be there stating, "I worked hard all my life to not be in such a place." She quit eating. Visiting her was painful. Overcome with sadness, I remember slumping to the floor outside her room after seeing my mother, once active, now listless.

A few weeks later, my dad called saying "You'd better come home. She's dying." I went back to Pennsylvania willing to try anything to keep my mother alive. Wisely, my dad said, "She's been through enough. Leave her alone". He took me to visit his friend, a priest, who calmed me with his words about his own mother's last days. The minister of Mother's church prayed with her and she seemed to relax. She died the next morning. I spent time arranging the funeral with my dad. Mother had written out exactly what readings and music she wanted.

I called Bill and told him to come with the kids. He asked what clothes they should bring. I had thought about this and answered, "Look at the last formal portrait and have each bring what they wore." Bill was willing to bring back my mother's china for a luncheon after the funeral. The ladies from Mother's church wanted to host it, but Dad wouldn't go to their church. "Your mother always entertained here at the house," he said. For one last time, the ladies served her friends and family on Mother's china in her house.

I was proud of Bill for being accommodating, my family for their good behavior and the tributes shown my mother. I feel her presence often when I remember one of her Mom-isms, "Always act like you know what you are doing. White hair will get you everywhere" or "You can have things happen to you or make them happen." Bill and I do make things happen for our family by establishing traditions, Christmas morning photos with all sitting on steps, birthday dinners out and Sunday phone calls from those out of town.

The boys became tall teens. The whole family crowding in one room to watch TV seemed like the circus act of clowns stuffed in a tiny car. After adding a master suite over the garage, we lived on Heil Drive eight more years, using every bit of the house and the new space. We needed more room.

One day in September as Hilde arrives, the phone rings.

"Turn on your TV," my neighbor says.

"Hilde, come here," I scream.

We stand, stunned, in front of the TV to watch the horror of 911 unfold.

"This isn't a movie," I say. "This is an attack in our country."

Hilde shivers. "Like bombings in Germany."

"It's happening again!" Hilde yells.

"Why?" We stare at the screen and cry.

We listen to the announcer's voice full of emotion trying to make sense of what he sees.

"My cousin and a friend live in the city," I say. "I hope they are safe."

We both wonder aloud. "What's going to happen next?"

Hilde and I eat our lunches in front of the TV watching the aftermath of the fallen twin towers.

"What a loss of lives,' she says.

"Imagine being in one of those buildings and knowing you are going to die."

The TV stays on all day as we hear of the additional attempts, the heroics of the flight in Pennsylvania and the damage at the Pentagon.

We clean house watching TV and listening for further reports as we felt the enormity of the attacks, sorrow for the lives lost and fear of what will happen next.

We come to the same conclusion. There are people who really hate us!

Peg with Lee and Greg in evening visit to a Seattle beach while
Bill photographed trains and beautiful sunsets. 1970

Chapter Nineteen

1977-2002
Whitehall, Ohio

While the Mideast Peace Conference took place, the Berlin Wall came down and the New Millenium started, Bruni became Hilde.

While Bernie and I were separated, Peggy, my quiet fourteen-year-old, ran away. Worried senseless, I drove around all night looking for her and rang doorbells of school friends. None of them would tell me anything. Finally I found out she ran away with Claire. One day later the Circleville police, in a town south of Columbus, called to say that they found Peggy and Claire in a restroom at a gas station. I was told to pick up my daughter. Terrified to drive in the blizzard, I had to call Bernie for help. Claire's parents refused to get their daughter who had run away fifteen times. In snow and ice, we drove twenty miles to Circleville to get both girls. I let Bernie come back into my life. I could not handle this situation with Peggy alone. For awhile she stayed home until Bernie and I divorced in 1977.

Bernie bought a beautiful house with a down payment and all new furniture. I never could find out where he got the money. He was told by the judge to sell the motor home and the boat and pay all the debts. I was very sad when he moved out and Peggy ran away with Claire again. They hitch-hiked to West Virginia, got picked up by the highway patrol and put into the detention center in Columbus. From there she went to

Rosemont, a school for wayward girls in Columbus. They ran off again. She was gone for four months.

While Peggy was still missing, I moved to a condo in Whitehall, near the Columbus airport. Susi was upset that we moved. "It's a dump," she said. I replied, "It is not as nice as the house in Reynoldsburg with Bernie, but I'm grateful that I have a place to go and put a roof over my children's head." My friends didn't help matters. Some of them said, "You'll never get that condo. The bank is not going to give you a loan." I showed them!

I was cleaning a few houses and received Aid for Dependent Children. I decided to go to school. With help of grants from the state of Ohio, I got into a business college. With added money from the school's student aid, I was barely able to make ends meet. In two years I hoped to have an associate degree. Each day for the first few months, I would cry when I came home from school. Classes were hard to learn in English. I was frustrated. Some classes I had to repeat. It took me three years to finish.

Still I could not find a job with no job experience. At forty, I knew my age was also a reason. I went to many interviews and took test after test. I received a card in the mail from the state that I passed at 80-90% and would be notified. I never heard from the state or post office about a job. One company offered me a job at three dollars and seventy-five cents an hour. With three children at home, I couldn't take a job in graphic arts at that wage. I was making eight dollars per hour cleaning homes.

Meanwhile, Peggy did not know where I lived. When the phone or doorbell rang, my heart stopped and my knees went weak thinking the police were calling or at the door to let me know they found my daughter's body. I would not wish this horror on my worst enemy. One year from the first time she ran away from Rosemont my doorbell rang in the middle of the night. I opened the door and there was a shivering Peggy. "I want to come home", she said. "Friends told me where you moved. Claire deserted me and left me alone. I landed at Rosemont again." I had signed custody over to the state for I could not handle Peggy. She did not want to abide by my rules. When she came home finally, we went back to court and I regained custody again on probation. She stayed put and things got better.

Peggy went to school, always getting A's. At seventeen she started dating the boy next door. A month after graduation they got married. It was a nice small white wedding in church. I pleaded with her to wait. "Marriage is not a bowl of cherries," I told them. They paid all the expenses for a very nice wedding. They both had jobs. I liked my new son-in-law. To my shock, Peggy came home six months later. Her husband was running around with his ex-fiancé and she had a new boyfriend. I was devastated.

Susi did well during her teen years, although she always back-talked and was stubborn. Things went well until she met her second boyfriend when she was twenty. I was upset for she had moved out again to live with this man who was twelve years older. "He has a past with women and babies," I told Susi. She would not listen. Her boss told me that one day she came to work as an executive secretary with two black eyes. I begged and pleaded with her "You've got to leave him." She screamed at me, "You are jealous because you don't have a man. You're crazy. You belong in the nut house on the hilltop". I often could not understand why my daughters treated me this way. I sacrificed so much. We lived in poverty and I tried so hard to hold my family together. I loved my girls then and I still love them. By then, Susi and Peggy were fourteen and fifteen and started working, one at MacDonalds and the other at the swimming pool. When Susi turned eighteen and had a job as an executive secretary, I asked her to pay room and board. Peggy, at eighteen, was working at the public library. I wanted them to help me and pay room and board so I could get job experience and advance to a better position, but to no avail. Susi wanted to move in with her boyfriend and Peggy married the boy next door.

Susi had excellent grades and went to a vocational high school. She won first place at a beauty contest combined with her achievements, she got hired at OEA, Ohio Education Association, as an executive secretary. My daughter went to conventions and stayed at nice hotels. She was treated like a lady. She bought a nice car and lived at home, but she was not happy. She was living with Peter and became pregnant. Peter choked her and beat her. She finally left him and stayed at CHOICES, a women's shelter. I brought her money for gasoline and diapers. I had to meet her at a park for I was not to know where CHOICES was located.

At that time, I was cleaning one man's house to make extra money. Every other week I cleaned his beautiful home. He was very kind to me. He invited me to his party one Sunday. I talked to a nice lady and she asked me about Germany and why I hadn't been back there since 1973. I told her I was penniless and mentioned that I had a daughter and son-in-law and grandson in Germany that I had not seen or met in eleven years.

I received a call from my sweet male friend, Richard. He asked me why I had not told him that I had a daughter and her family in Germany. "I do not tell my clients my private business," I said. Mr. Hamilton told me to get a piece of paper and pen to write down two flights to Germany for three weeks another for five weeks. I said "Why? I am not going to Germany."

He said "Oh yes you are. I am sending you."

Shocked, I sat down and started laughing and screaming. My girls came downstairs and asked what was wrong. I was almost delirious from joy and disbelief. Mr. Hamilton laughed on the phone and told me to settle down. I went a week later to clean his house he told me to apply for a passport. I was broke, so I told him I would get one as soon as I had fifty dollars. As he went to work, he drove by the front door and reached out and handed me a fifty dollar bill. "Get a passport", he said. It was like Christmas in July!

When my flight left from Columbus, he came to the airport to make sure I got on the plane. He was always so grateful when I cleaned for him and helped him at his parties. I offered to send a girlfriend to clean for him while I was gone, but he declined. He wanted only me.

One year after I came back his leg suddenly swelled up and he was diagnosed with an aneurysm. He was a Christian Scientist and did not go to the doctor or hospital. When his life partner finally admitted him to the hospital, it was too late. He died at six a.m. on an October Sunday. He was sixty-two. Devastated, I cried for days. I still carry his picture in my wallet, for I loved that dear, kind man.

In Germany 1984 things had changed. My daughter Petra and husband had a restaurant with a bed and breakfast and a very nice beer garden. My mother-in-law's live-in boyfriend, Joseph, had passed away in 1971. My daughter Petra inherited their house. My son-in-law is an excellent chef. When I was there, customers waited outside in line on the sidewalk to eat at Petra's. Her *Vater* Heinz, my ex, had died at thirty-six of alcoholism. My *Vater* Ludwig died in 1975 of a heart attack. I was glad to have gone to Germany in 1973 to see him one last time.

When my daughter, Petra, was thirty she became pregnant again against doctor's orders. She had miscarried once, and this pregnancy was touch and go. She spent most of her time in bed until Sarah was born. She is the only girl among boy cousins. The in-laws were ecstatic and, to this day, Sarah is spoiled by all the relatives.

Back in Columbus, at CHOICES, Susi had saved all her money, went job hunting and rented an apartment far from me. Peter did not know where. He wrote me threatening letters and warned me if I did not tell him where Susi was, something terrible would happen to the rest of my family. I reported this to the police and showed them the letters. My beautiful Susi would not take my advice. I provided her with furniture and household goods for the apartment. She had a good job and she had a daughter, Rachel.

She got involved with another low-life who smoked pot. Ralph had two children who lived with him. Soon Susi was pregnant again. When Ralph was mean to Rachel, Susi broke off the relationship. My grandson, Jordan was born. She decided to go back to Peter. He was looking for her and was only too happy to have her back.

They married and the beatings began again. Susi was not working and she was not calling. Peter totally isolated her. Jordan was three-years-old, when Susi decided also to go into the Army hoping the military would protect her from her husband. Home on leave, she was beaten again, her nose broken and she landed in the hospital. Two days later she was on her way to Monterey, California with her two children where she had to report for duty. She never called me and told me about the beating and hospital stay. Peter went to jail and got out on bail. Nothing came of this for Susi could not come to court. She was on her way to California. She got a divorce from Peter in that state.

At that time, Patty had turned eighteen and decided to be a policewoman. She joined the US Air Force and went to Texas for boot camp.

At the same time, her older sister, Peggy, joined the Air Force in 1985 and was stationed in Arizona. One day Peggy called me saying that she had gotten married to a co-worker. Sometime later she called saying

"He tied me to a chair and terrorized me for hours, choked me into unconsciousness, then gave me a chance to get away. He had planned to kill me. I ran to a neighbor. She called the police. Jeff was arrested for attempted murder and later committed suicide." Traumatized, my daughter could not stay alone. The Air Force contacted her sister, Patty in Texas, and sent her to stay with Peggy for a month. They asked me to stay with her but I had no money to travel.

Peggy recovered and moved after that ordeal. She was stationed in England and traveled to Switzerland, Wales and Scotland. Peggy also went to Germany to my hometown to visit her oldest sister Petra. They had a wonderful time. I was very happy to hear that my girls got together. Peggy loved the German food. The language was no barrier for my son-in-law Jürgen and my grandson, Kai, spoke fluent English. Petra was so happy to finally see one of her sisters. My ex mother-in-law Maria, Petra's grandmother, waited on Peggy hand and foot. Jürgen and Kai were smitten with Peggy. "A beautiful American Girl" they called her.

Two years later, Peggy was transferred to New Mexico where she met her next soldier-husband Kevin. They had a daughter Raven and another nightmare began.

***

In 1985 I became a United States citizen. I had been in the states for 22 years, and wanted to stay where I had raised my children. I was surprised how easy it was to gain citizenship! I applied and studied the information, went to the courthouse and answered correctly questions about the Constitution, a few laws and could name the President and Vice President. I signed some papers, was sworn in and certified as a citizen. It was a bitter-sweet day, becoming a citizen of a country where I had lived longer than in my home country.

Suzi, in California, decided to look for her father. After several phone calls she found him living in Tennessee working for Dolly Parton in Dollywood. She wanted answers from him for all the years she missed him and cried for him wanting to know why he left her. YJ was speechless on the phone, and then came up with all kinds of excuses.

Susi was so excited and happy to have found her father. She wanted to share the good news with me. I received her phone call and she told me how the reunion came about. I was all right with the news. She told me what was said in their conversation. She needed to know what the situation was years ago. Then she suggested that her father and I should become friends and forget everything. I was crying when the conversation started, but the idea of friendship was too much.

I went crazy, absolutely crazy. I screamed and cried into the phone. I tried to make it clear to Susi. "Don't you dare bring him into my house. I swear I will kill him." I told her I had a gun and I would use it.

I was told, "Oh Mom, you don't mean that."

I screamed again. I shook with sobs and told her again, "Don't bring him around. I'll go to prison for him. I do not care." I ended the conversation and tried to calm myself. I know Susi was disappointed but I was not willing to go along with her crazy thinking. I know that she told YJ what I said. I didn't care.

She decided to leave the Army after four years. Life was expensive in Monterey and she never had money. She did not earn much with two children to support. She told her father she was coming to Tennessee to be near him. When she called him to let him know when she was coming, YJ quit his job and moved with his wife and kids to North Carolina. Susi should have realized that her father did not want her. He was afraid that I would find out and the law would go after him for non-support.

Grandma Gunter gave Susi his new address and phone number. Susi then moved to North Carolina with Rachel and Jordan. "I was deliriously happy to finally find him and be with him. I accused him of things and reprimanded him for leaving us".

YJ told Susi, "Bruni was a good wife and mother but we didn't get along".

Susi got a job and was fired because they did not like her to take time away for Reserve duty in the Army. She found another job, but quit the Reserve for fear she'd get fired again.

YJ had a friend named Walt. He was a total alcoholic and sixteen-years-older than Susi. She started dating him and they moved in together. She had no common sense. I'm convinced she had no brain when it came to men. YJ was upset "You're going to get hurt, girl. Walt is no good," he told her. Susi feeling bitter towards her father, laughed in his face and said, "No man hurt me like you did. You are the only man who hurt me. You left me" When she asked YJ for two thousand dollars for a down payment on a house, he refused. Yet he had received sixty thousand dollars in profit sharing from Dollywood when he quit there.

One day Walt asked YJ "How could you bring a German girl over here from Germany and leave her pregnant with two other children?"

YJ told him, "Patty is not my daughter. Bruni got pregnant too quick after I came home from Vietnam. No woman gets pregnant that fast." Walt told Susi and hell broke loose. She was shocked.

Walt and Susi came to Ohio to visit me and Susi told me what YJ said. I was speechless. When Patty got up from bed and came down stairs, Walt said, "My God, she is the spitting image of YJ." Susi looked Patty over to convince herself that Patty was her real sister. After we told her of what her father had said, Patty told Walt "You can tell him any father is better than him."

Walt and Susi broke up and she met a man named David and married him. Susi is now estranged from her father. She realized that he had not changed. Susi and I had a huge argument with her blaming me for all of her mistakes and for her father leaving us.

***

As the Wall came down in Germany in 1989, many foreigners came to Germany. They stole and plundered, broke into people's homes. They stole cars and drove them to East Germany and *Tschecloslavakia* to paint then change the license plates. I don't think it was a good idea to tear the Wall down. The East Germans did not have anything and were extremely poor and wanted to finally have food and clothing, TV's and microwaves. After forty years of living behind the Wall in poverty, then freedom, the East Germans took over. West Germans didn't go out shopping anymore any longer for the East Germans were very rude. To this day, West Germans still have to pay high taxes to rebuild East Germany and *Tschecheslovakia,* the damage that Hitler and the Nazis created during WWII. My country had changed drastically while I was gone.

In 1990 I made another trip to Germany. I did not get to see my brother, Helmut. He had moved and the relatives did not know where to locate him. He had not married and liked to party. No one offered to find him.

On that same trip in 1990 I visited with my *Vater's* second wife, Agnes. As we were talking, she asked me about an incident that happened a few years ago. She had met an acquaintance who stated that now that my *Vater* was dead, this man could talk about it. He told his wife about my *Vater* shooting at my mother, her lover and her children. Agnes was shocked and told him she didn't believe him. "It's a lie!" she shouted. "I have lived with Ludwig in this town for thirty years. No body ever told me about that."

I acknowledged that the story was true and my mother was sent to a concentration camp. I admitted, too, that my *Vater* and my grandmother were responsible for that terrible ordeal. Agnes and her friend looked at me with their mouths wide open. Agnes, then cried and yelled, "I was married to the devil. How could he do that? He was the devil and no one told me. I had my share of problems with him too with his drinking, but I loved him." She turned to me in tears, "I am so sorry, Bruni."

In 1995 I was working night shift in a Columbus hospital as a nursing assistant. I was living alone and did not know the German authorities had tried to contact me. Because of the time difference, they could not reach me by phone. I did not come home until eight or nine in the morning. Finally my daughter Petra called me one Saturday afternoon to give me the news. "Helmut's been missing for four months. One day city workers were cleaning debris around the River Röslau. They found a body hung inside a pipe in the river. He was unrecognizable and wearing only jeans and red socks. Only from dental records could they identify him as Helmut. He worked at a restaurant and trained horses. The employees did not report him missing. His landlady put his belongings out on the curb. The authorities found out that he had gone to the bank to withdraw money. That was the last anyone saw of him."

I was shocked and saddened that I did not see my brother for many years. The Germans demanded that I pay for my brother's funeral expenses for I was his blood sister. I had no money so they buried him in a pauper's grave. My brother Helmut had a very sad childhood and life similar to mine.

Back in Columbus Ohio, cleaning houses became a full-time job with steady weekly customers. I made more money cleaning houses than working in the hospital as a nursing assistant. I kept in touch with my German roots by joining and attending activities at the Germania Club in Columbus' German Village.

In the twelve years I cleaned for the Hanna's from 1989-2002, lunchtime conversations continued with the sharing of lives past and present. I revisited my hometown for a school reunion, stayed with my family and brought photos to help describe the town. Mrs. Hanna and I shared opinions on current events, discussed books we'd read, expressed ideas on child-rearing and bragged about grandchildren. By then I was grandmother to Susi's Rachel and Jordan, Petra's Kai and Sarah and Peggy's Raven. I have tried to stay in touch with all of them.

I obtained my cousin's verification of my mother's concentration camp experience and retrieved photos of my younger years. I spent many hours writing about my German life after phone calls to my family and friends.

And WHILE began.

Chapter Twenty

1987-2002
Gahanna, Ohio

While the Persian Gulf War began, San Francisco Earthquake occurred, and Y2K scare covered the world, Peg and her family changed drastically.

We bought a bigger house a mile away. We had watched it being built and never dreamed it would fit us one day. The Dutch colonial had been built for a family with six boys and one girl. Seventeen years later, our family of five boys and one girl fit perfectly. The children could stay in the same schools. We could stay in the same parish.

We moved in December 1987. Lee, home from college, had his wisdom teeth pulled, and during recovery, helped with the move. We quickly made friends with neighbors who greeted us with, "We are happy to see small children in the neighborhood again". At the same time, Bill went on a two-week business trip to Japan. While he was gone, the children and I moved in. I told them, "We'll put Pop's things where we think they should go. He'll have to find them when he comes home."

Mother had died that fall and my dad was coming out for Christmas. Not only did I have the stress of arranging our things in a new house, I had to get ready for the holiday. The choice of bedrooms had been decided and the older boys put theirs in order. They helped me arrange the younger one's rooms. A good friend came and helped me put away my china. As only children Bill and I had inherited my mother's and grandmother's china and stemware, as well as Bill's mother's, his grandmother's and Aunt Bea's. We have a set of china for each of our children for when they marry.

The boys and I baked for the holidays. Bill and I had made the traditional fruitcake the day after Thanksgiving. The children and I followed our weekly routine for grocery shopping. The younger children cut out coupons. After dropping Lee off at the doctors for his allergy shot, I drove to the grocery store. Greg and one child took a cart and did coupon shopping. I took the others and a cart and bought staples. Jay stayed home and directed putting things away. We could finish shopping in an hour, pick up Lee and be home in time to store groceries and fix dinner.

Roy turned four that winter. Kristin, a first grader, spent days in her room ill with pneumonia. My lively little girl lay limp as the Pound Puppy she constantly hugged. I "home-schooled" her for eight weeks. Stephen, a third grader, would bring her day's assignments home and take back completed work. Kristin was caught up to her classmates when she returned to school. Each week I took her to the doctor's for blood work. When he would say, "Stay home another week", Kristin and I would both cry, then say, "Let's go to MacDonald's. A milkshake will make us feel better!"

At the same time we were redecorating the house. Roy and the wallpaper man became good friends. Roy would sit on the steps and talk to John while I tutored Kristin. We could hear their constant conversation, "What are you doing? Why are you standing on a board? Will you fall?" John would patiently answer Roy and continue working.

We celebrated our twenty-fifth wedding anniversary the summer of '89 with a mass at our parish church, followed by a dinner catered at our house. My childhood friend and bridesmaid, Joyce came from Maryland and Bill's best man, Jim came from Pennsylvania. With one hundred people at the house, we felt happy and proud of our new home, family and friendships. We played "Peg&Bill Trivia" testing how well our friends knew us. Family and friends came from five states to celebrate. At midnight, storms left the neighborhood without power.

The caterers and the immediate family washed dishes by candlelight. We were too tired and happy to complain.

Greg started college that fall. He lived on campus at a nearby college and continued to work at Bob Evans restaurant on weekends. We wanted the children to experience living away from home. When he left for college the family dynamics changed again. Jay became the oldest at home. When asked why I was sad at Greg's leaving as I already had Lee away from home, I replied "I miss Greg's sense of humor". It was Jay's time to shine as he was now the oldest at home.

My father came to live with us the next summer when he had open-heart surgery. We agreed that it was better for him to have the quadruple bypass in Columbus where I could help with his recuperation. Yet the day he arrived, he got a taste of our life. Roy was hit in the forehead with a brick! Screaming, he ran into the house with his face covered in blood. My dad went white. My maternal instincts took over. I scooped up Roy and called Bill. "Meet us at Children's Hospital," I said then turned to a friend who had come to visit. "Please stay with Dad, Kristin and Stephen". Roy's forehead required nine stitches. Bill asked the doctor how many children he stitched a day. When he said, "That's all I do," we gave him permission to stitch up our son.

Dad grew to know the children that summer, play cards and watch baseball games with them and share family stories. He went home after three months, lived two more years alone, then came back to live with us, but was hospitalized with pneumonia and died six weeks later. "I want three things before I die," he said. "To sell my house, see big city doctors and see the grandkids again". He did all three and lives on in our second son, Greg, who has his personality. He never knows a stranger.

An unexpected phone call one morning brought the news that my childhood friend Joyce had been killed in a car accident in Maryland. Devastated, I swallowed my fear of flying and flew there alone to be with her family. Joyce and I had grown up together, been in each others weddings, godparents to each other's children and in close contact through our adult life. I asked to read from Scripture at her funeral. I wanted to do one final thing for "my sister".

Treated as family, I was comforted in the arms of her husband, mother and brother. In our sorrow, we laughed about incidents from our Polk Street years, shared our grown up lives and cried for our loss. When back home, I wrote a poem for Joyce, an outlet for my pain. Entitled "In Winter" I concluded with the lines,

> "After many winters
> Photographs bring her back.
> Her family grows and changes.
> She remains alive in her children
> Their faces are hers
> Every winter."

At that time Bruni, Hilde as we know her now, came to clean house for the family. Lee was home finishing his college years at Ohio State University, Greg was at Capital University and Jay was in high school. The three younger ones were elementary school. Hilde's help was needed. Our lunchtime discussions started. We were amazed that we had knee injuries in childhood, she had a daughter with my name, and later when I was still going to college, she had been married twice and had two children.

In the following years, our family hosted ten exchange students and one teacher, Anne-Laure from France, Lone from Denmark, Leo from Venezuela, Carmen from Peru, Anne and Leo from Germany and Marta and Iniake from Spain, Katia, a teacher from Chile and Elizabeth a graduate intern from Texas. I have been their Ohio Mom while our children were teens and could introduce them to American high school experiences and their friends.

Three of their families came to celebrate Christmases with our family. We enjoyed their company, introduced them to American customs and continue to correspond with them. All three families were impressed with American's traditions. "You have so many outdoor lights!" "You have too many presents!" "Why do you bake so many cookies?" The French family teased me about my bread machine from Santa. They couldn't get enough of the "electric bread". I baked a loaf for them every meal.

Our son Jay was an exchange student in Germany the year after his high school graduation. It was hard to put him on the plane and know we wouldn't see him for a school year. Hilde was cleaning for us then and enjoyed Jay's letters from Germany. "Les Miserables", the stage play, was popular at that time. I couldn't bear to hear the song "Bring Him Home" without crying. I missed my son.

Bill and I visited him near the end of his stay. We met and toured with his host family in Kühlungsborn, met our Danish student's parents in Berlin and stayed with our French student's family in Lyon. We toured Germany by train with Jay who could speak the language. Investigating the Leis family roots there was disappointing. Records were burned in their hometown. There was no information available. We have heard many times from our exchange students and three have visited when they were in this country again. We visit often with the Texan. Again, our children learned how much people are alike than different. They have not been afraid to travel and see the world.

Lee married in 1991 after he and Eileen had graduated from OSU. We met Eileen one December evening when Bill and I asked Lee to come home from OSU and babysit for an annual business event. "Could I bring someone with me?" he asked. From then on, he and Eileen dated, and Eileen came for Sunday dinners. One fall Sunday dinner they announced their engagement. I knew it was coming, but expected it at Christmastime. Bill's Aunt Bea had given Lee his great-grandmother's engagement ring and he couldn't wait to give Eileen the diamond. They had a beautiful wedding in our church. Eileen's parents had moved while she was in college and she had attended church with us. Their wedding was planned in three-way conversations with Eileen, her mother and Lee. Eileen was working off the coast of Washington at the time. Lee and I scouted out photographers and places for the reception. People commented to me, "You didn't cry during the wedding." My response was "I was happy that it all came together."

For their honeymoon, Lee and Eileen took the same cross-country train trip to the Northwest as Lee had with us when younger. Eileen had worked out of Seattle and they both revisited places they knew. We were pleased that Lee's childhood experience became part of his new life. This was a new stage of our life, our first was married. I became a mother-in-law and felt grateful that Eileen immediately called me "Mom".

We waited seven years to become grandparents. Will, William Swan Hanna was named in the family tradition with Eileen's maiden name.

Bill and I entered another stage of life and love seeing the first son of our first son.

When our three younger ones were teens, we took the train cross-country to San Diego first on business with Bill, enjoyed an exciting stay at Disneyworld, visited Los Angeles and wide-eyed, toured Hollywood. We came home the southern route and waved to people white-water rafting on the Colorado River, viewed impressive towers of red rocks jutting out of the land, and returned to flat farmlands as we entered the Midwest. Our children made friends onboard, toured California with business friends and their children and experienced traveling by train again.

We returned many times to Edinboro Lake in Pennsylvania where Bill and I met. His parents retired and Dad built a house at the head of the lake. He built the one-floor brick house except for the pouring of the basement cement and installation of the furnace. We went back on vacations and Bill helped his father complete the house. We spent many happy summer vacations there with the children, relaxing, swimming in the lake, traveling into Erie and visiting friends. My college roommates Betty Ann and Laurie lived nearby. When Bill's parents died, they left the house to us. Bill's Aunt Bea lived there for us until she died.

We tried to keep the property and house, but had to sell when we couldn't go back often, pay taxes in two states and rent it to unknowns. It was a bittersweet decision. Lee and Eileen had just bought a house in Columbus and took most of the furniture. We took what we wanted and arranged for an auction for the remaining items. The house sold quickly. We have gone back and it's hard to see it changed from what Dad had built. Bill and I had let go of the place where we met and ended another Hanna chapter.

Our faith and family were tested when Stephen, at fourteen, announced that he is gay. His brothers and sisters knew before we did. Bill and I, shaken, didn't know how to respond other than to say, "You are and always will be a part of this family." We sought counseling and expressed our fears and concerns and were reassured that we were doing the right thing by not turning our backs on our son. We had no association with gays and had heard only negative comments about their lifestyle. I was afraid Stephen would be beaten and left to die on a football field. We have accepted the fact that he is gay and proud to hear that he has counseled others.

Our faith was tested again when one of our grandsons was born with Infantile Fibromatosis. Lee and Eileen's second son spent his three-and-one half month life in and out of the hospital. David's little body, full of tumors, could not survive. His short life strengthened our family in love and support. Friendships and prayers gave us appreciation and new respect for life. I was in contact with people all over the nation gaining information online about this rare disease and presenting it to the doctors. The family took turns staying with David while he was hospitalized. I tearfully held him as he was given the church's Blessing of the Sick and again realized how fragile life is. At his funeral, I placed a miniature rocking chair with him. I had rocked him at every visit in the hospital. As one of my friends said, "David knew he was loved." Will, two at the time, remembers David "as a visitor". Lee and Eileen took a great leap of faith and had another child. Thomas has no signs of the disease.

I had been teaching a creative writing class at the senior center in Gahanna. From a chance comment by one of the seniors, Bill and I flew to Ireland. This senior had been to Ireland seventeen times and stated "The center's trip would be a good one". We joined others in a memorable flight and bus tour through the southern part of the country. Photos show us standing before the many shades of green countryside. We stayed in a castle overnight, overlooked the Atlantic from the Cliffs of Moher, kissed the Blarney Stone,(Bill says I already have the gift of gab) viewed the Book of Kells in Dublin, toured the Waterford Crystal factory and enjoyed shepherd's pie and evening life in Killarney pubs. We hope one day to return and visit the northern parts of the country, the home of Bill's and my ancestors. I bought and still wear an authentic Irish cable knit wool sweater, one remembrance of the wonderful trip.

In Ireland on the first anniversary of 9/11, we attended two memorial services. We were handed American flags by our tour director as we departed the bus for the cathedrals. We were proud to carry them. An Irish woman approached Bill and asked for one of the flags. She explained that her husband was an American living in Ireland and didn't have an American flag. Bill was very happy to give her his flag. After the very moving services, as we stood outside, the Irish extended their sympathies for American's losses. We thanked them and reciprocated with our thanks as many of the first responders were Irish-American firemen and police.

***

Our children were active in school organizations and sports and worked through high school years. If they wanted to drive, they had to work for gas money. We held many teen parties and "overnights" at our house. The kids' friends always ask "Mrs. H, do you still bake on Saturdays?" and "Would you make brownies when we visit?"

We have been band parents, scout parents, play cast parents, cross country and wrestling parents. We have allowed our children to come back home temporarily "in between" school and jobs. We want to provide a stable, loving place to come and regroup, then move on. Bill teases me saying "You're happiest when household is full of people." I love to cook and entertain. I identify with a quote from "I Am Invisible" posted nationally on the internet.

"When I really think about it, I don't want my son to tell the friend he's bringing home from college for Thanksgiving, 'My mom gets up at 4 in the morning and bakes homemade pies, and then she hand bastes a turkey for three hours and presses all the linens for the table.' That would mean I'd built a shrine or a monument to myself. I just want him to want to come home. And then, if there is anything more to say to his friend, to add, 'You're gonna love it there'."

At one of our last lunchtimes together, I say "It's unbelievable but we have another connection."

"Oh?" says Hilde.

"Getting out my mother's china to use for dessert, I noticed the seal on the back."

"So?'

"It was marked Bavarian from Arzberg, your town." I almost shout.

"Was it marked Schumann?"

I nod. "Why?"

"That was the factory owner's name. My step grandfather Simon, worked in that factory and drove the horse and carriage for the Schumann family."

Hilde smiles. "Every New Year's Day we would go to his house. He would give us money wishing us a Happy New Year."

I show Hilde the plate which held an indentation for a matching cup.

"I recognize the Wild Rose pattern," she smiles and says. "I worked in that factory, too."

"What part did you paint?"

"The gold rim only."

Hilde shakes her head. "The factory is gone now."

"Just like my hometown," I say. "The steel mill is gone, too."

Hilde sighs. "On my last trip back I saw the empty space where the buildings sat."

"I can't drive along the Ohio River in Aliquippa," I say. "It hurts to see the empty space where the mill stood."

"It's sad," we say in unison.

We eat our lunches in silence that day—remembering.

Hanna's larger house where Hilde cleaned house for the family from 1989-2002. Here is where lunchtime discussions started and Peg and Hilde collaborated on writing contrasting memoirs. 1989 photo

EPILOGUE

Bruni/Hilde

In 2003 YJ's wife passed away after being on oxygen for over twenty years. She was only fifty-four years old. YJ has had major heart attacks and lives somewhere in North Carolina. I received several checks of retroactive child support but they soon stopped coming. During this time I made a living cleaning houses, cleaning for steady customers for many years.

In 1990's I was surprised with a visit from David who visited me in Columbus while here on business. We shared many memories of our days in Georgia thirty-five years earlier. He remembered the two older girls and wanted to meet Patty.

Although I remarried, the love for my new husband was different. We had love and happiness for a little while, but in my heart I knew twenty years later, the love for my children's father was real and could only happen once in a lifetime. No matter how many relationships I could have had with eligible men, it would have never been the same. To this day, years later there is always a hollow empty space within me and a pain whenever I think of him, the father of my children, my children are so tall and so much like him in looks and demeanor. Nevertheless, I am still very proud of my daughters for they have achieved many things, are independent, honest and responsible.

The one consolation and joy I feel is "the apple of my eye" my youngest daughter, Patty. I never once had any trouble with her. She was obedient growing up, always respectful and trustworthy. At fifteen, she got a license to be a lifeguard and put all of her money into the bank. At eighteen, she joined the Air Force and was stationed in the Philippines, Texas and Mississippi. After four years she came home. She was a sergeant policewoman in the Air Force. She moved in with me and worked as security guard at the Columbus airport. She was not happy there. After attending a job fair, she applied at the Sheriff's department. Having been in the military helped her get the job. She finally got hired as a Deputy Sheriff. She bought a new car and a house with a pool in Columbus.

One day I went shopping in Columbus and a car collided with mine. When the police arrived, a tall young man in uniform named Roland gave the man a citation. It must have been destiny. I felt very close to the policeman. We talked. I introduced Patty to the officer and six years later they got married. I love my son-in-law. He is very special. I pray they will always stay together for they are good for each other.

I realized that life is very unfair and no matter how you sacrifice for your children, some of them do not feel gratitude.

Yet I have been welcome in each of my visits to my oldest daughter Petra and her family in Germany. She has often asked me to come and live with her. We know this is impossible, too many changes would have to be made. I have many wonderful friends and acquaintances in my new country, my home for over forty years.

Suzi has not called or written to me for over twelve years.

Peggy has married five times, left Columbus, I assume, to forget about the past. As of this date, after retiring from the Air Force with twenty-two years of service, she has made her home in another state. I am still at a loss as to what happened between Peggy and me. I am certain her last husband wanted to separate her from family. Many times I cry for the years gone by and memories lost. We have heard that she wants no contact with me and her sister Patty. I cannot call my granddaughter Raven. They have disconnected the phone.

I am satisfied that my daughters are all right. I do wish them the best and I love them with all my heart. I miss them.

Patty is the one daughter I know will be there if I should need her. Patty and I both know that she was born for a reason. I think God knew that my other daughters were going to desert me and let me have my Patty.

From one of my late customers, Mrs. Sharon Rea, I received a sizable gift. I wept when I received it. I had no idea I meant so much to this wonderful lady. I used the money for mortgage payments. I still maintain their house for Mr. Rea.

I live alone in Whitehall, Ohio now after many heartaches, loneliness and hardships, I have finally reached a chapter in my life where I have peace of mind and am satisfied with my life. I am still working. I no longer clean for the Hannas.

I pray to God to let me stay healthy and live in peace.

EPILOGUE

Peg

Four of our six children have graduated from college, two have a Masters degree, one a doctorate, one an actor, another, an Eagle Scout and Marine. Four are married and have given us six grandchildren. We see them often as the Sunday dinner rule still applies at least for once a month. Our neighbors on Heil Drive used to tease us and say, "If the Hannas didn't have a roast on Sunday night at six o'clock, their house would fall down". Our exchange students remember Sunday dinners, call and come for dinner when in town. Their calls of concern for our safety on 9/11 touched us deeply.

We have survived Bill's and my various surgeries. The summer of Bill's four eye surgeries, he wasn't to read and spent time in the basement wiring his model railroad. It saved our marriage. We weren't used to spending twenty-four hours a day together.

For our fortieth wedding anniversary, Bill and I toured Alaska by train and took our first cruise. It was exciting to see another part of our country a different way.

The same summer, Greg and Nancy were married. It was a proud day for both families. Bride and groom were in their early thirties and had waited a long time to find each other.

Most of our children and grandchildren live in Columbus. Greg and Nancy and their daughter Ruthie and son, Evan, live in Chicago. Kristin lives in Toledo where, now as a doctor of Occupational Therapy, she works in a rehab center.

Bill and I babysit our grandchildren, Will and Thomas, when possible either in our home or theirs. We travel to Toledo and Chicago often. Kristin and Greg call home Sunday evenings and the phone is passed around the dinner table.

Our youngest son, Roy, joined the United States Marine Corps immediately out of high school. After training, he was deployed to Iraq. Before he left, he married his girlfriend Whitney. Roy has returned safely from a second tour in Iraq. He and Whitney have a little boy, Gavin and baby girl, Brooklynn. We are "back-up" for their present day-time babysitter while Roy and Whitney work.

Our oldest Lee, has been a stay-at-home dad to his two boys and, at one time, watched Gavin while Roy and Whitney worked. One day, Greg's daughter Ruthie, climbed on Lee's lap with a book for him to read. Not hearing her daddy's voice, she stared up at Lee who responded, "Don't worry. I'm a professional." The family sense of humor lives.

A few years ago, our good friends, Bea and her husband Dave, died of cancer within a year of each other. I felt the same knife slice through my body as I did when Bea held my hand and announced that they were moving to Memphis. I had lost another "sister". I concluded my eulogy with reading the last line one of my poems Bea had liked.

"If memory is a rope of sand,
Is every beach a diary?"
And added "May we meet again on that beach".

***

When our only daughter married, she had an informal wedding in Toledo. It was fun to help Kristin choose a gown as I hadn't had that experience. Her five brothers "roasted" Kristin at the reception, telling stories about her growing up years. All six ended with a group hug.

Jay lives in Columbus and is keeping the Hanna name alive at Battelle. He is an archivist. Stephen works part time at a Columbus restaurant and performs in local theater productions.

Lynn, Elaine, Carolee and I meet annually, email and phone each other often.

Bill and I continue to be active. Bill retired after thirty-four years at Battelle, works part time in a store selling model trains and volunteers for Habitat for Humanity. I have written and published reading books with an educational publisher and fiction with an independent publisher. Enrolled in Program Sixty classes at the Ohio State University, I took classes in writing poetry and fiction. I volunteer at a local hospital and belong to writer's groups, a prayer group, a book club and a woman's Euchre club. Keeping active is important to me. My mother said it keeps the "cobwebs from forming in the brain".

My philosophy of life is from my mother. "You can have things happen to you or you can make things happen."

While Bruni's and my lives have been different, they have made interesting contrasts in personalities, family life and personal struggles.

Notes

Chapter 1

1. After the war, at ten, I ate my first banana. Imported fruits had been unavailable during wartime blockades. "The banana's curved shape and mild taste fascinated me. Can I eat the whole thing?" I asked wide-eyed. "I don't have to share it?"

2. Ration cards used during the war were printed starting in 1939. Initially, people were allotted 2700 calories per day. Ration periods lasted four weeks. Everything had a patriotic names.

3. Jews and Poles in occupied Germany received lower rations. Jews were issued cards with a small purple "j". Shop owners were ordered to serve them last. At the end of the day, shop owners glued the collected *Marken* to a large sheet of paper and turn into the authorities. Whipped cream, chocolates and cakes with heavy creams were unknown from 1939-1948. Meat was not eaten every day. *Marken* for meat would be used for whatever meat available that day, pork, veal and sometimes horsemeat. People waited in lines for hours to cash in their stamps.

   Clothing was also rationed with a *Kleiderkarte*. Donated items were available and bought with points. Families would go to city centers when their homes were bombed and all was lost. There they would find clothes for the family. A teenage girl might leave the clothing center wearing the only item left, a man's jacket.

4. After the war, we found out that the landlord, a Nazi, hosted SS meetings in that restaurant.

Chapter 2

5. Dad was thirty-six when the Selective Service Act was enacted in 1940, requiring all men between the ages of twenty and thirty-six to serve one year to eighteen months in the United States military (the draft).

6. Certain numbers were used to buy items, such as leather for shoes, sugar meat and butter. Sugar and coffee were the first foods rationed. For sugar, stamp No. 30 of book four for five pounds Jan. 16 – Mar. 31, for fuel oil No. 2 coupons, 10 gallons per unit through Mar.31. For shoes, Airplane stamp No. 1 Book 3 was good for one pair indefinitely. There were no nylon stockings for ladies. Nylon was used for making parachutes. Gas was rationed by stickers on car windshields. Letters indicated gallon allowances depending on owner's occupation. Black A's stood for non-essential driving 4 gallons per week, B, blue, for business and essential driving to war effort 8 gallons per week. C was for green, for commercial, physicians, ministers, mail carriers and railroad workers, T, blue, for truckers 5 gallons per week, R for farmers non-highway traffic and X for Congressmen and VIPS. A thirty-five mile per hour speed limit was imposed as Victory Speed. The back of the stamp book read, "IMPORTANT: When you have used your ration, salvage the TIN CANS and WASTE FATS. They are needed to make munitions for our fighting men. Cooperate with your local Salvage Committee".

About the Authors

Margaret Leis Hanna (Peg), a former teacher, was born and raised in Aliquippa, Pennsylvania, graduated from Grove City College with graduate studies at the University of Pittsburgh and The Ohio State University. She is a published author of children's books, <u>Tricia and the Blue Cap</u>, <u>Canneh, the Reluctant Christmas Camel</u> and <u>Seeing Stars</u> (Sprite Press), and leveled readers for Zaner-Bloser Educational Publishers. Peg has taught creative writing classes, won awards for poetry and fiction and is a member of the Ohio Writer's Guild and Franklinton Writers. Peg is married, the mother of six and grandmother of six. She lives in Columbus, Ohio.

Brunhilde Maurer Barron is a survivor, born in Marktredwitz and raised in Arzberg, Germany. During high school years, she attended classes and worked in the Arzberg china factory. Married and divorced with a daughter, she worked as a nanny when she met and married an American soldier. In 1963, with her husband and their two daughters, she came to the United States. She worked various jobs in the States, divorced and remarried. Bruni/ Hilde has returned several times to her hometown and visited her remaining family. Hilde has four daughters and five grandchildren. She lives and works in Columbus, Ohio.